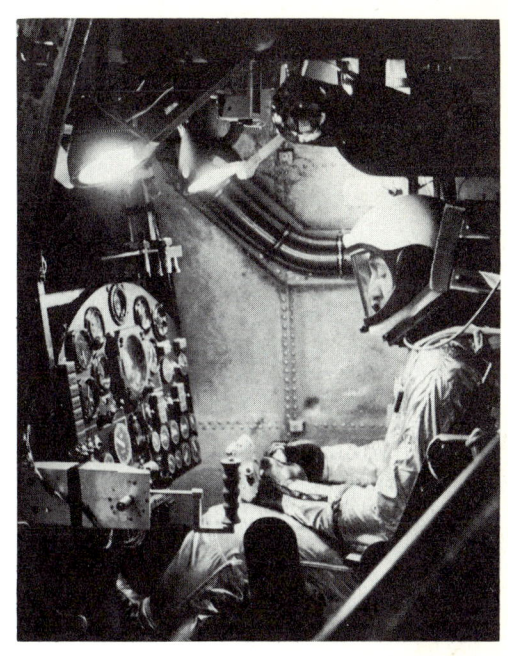

WHAT DOES AN ASTRONAUT DO?

OTHER BOOKS IN THIS SERIES

What Does a Civil Engineer Do?
What Does a Jet Pilot Do?
What Does a Parachutist Do?
What Does a Policeman Do?
What Does a Scientist Do?

WHAT DOES AN ASTRONAUT DO?

By Robert Wells
Foreword by Dr. John P. Hagen, NASA
Illustrated with photographs

DODD, MEAD & COMPANY
New York

To Jim, June, John and Jamie

Jacket drawing and illustrations on pages 12, 17, 20, 55 and 63 by Frank Tinsley, reproduced through the courtesy of American Bosch Arma Corporation

Copyright © 1961 by Robert L. Wells
All rights reserved
No part of this book may be reproduced in any form without permission in writing from the publisher
Library of Congress Catalog Card Number: 61-7033
Printed in the United States of America

FOREWORD

[Dr. John P. Hagen, former head of Project Vanguard, is Director of NASA's Office for the United Nations Conference and is responsible for planning, coordinating and directing United States participation in the First International Conference on the Peaceful Uses of Outer Space.]

The most exciting and daring single act that man has planned is his personal exploration of space. Man from the beginning has lived in a narrow region of space, in the lower and denser part of the atmosphere, above the surface of the earth and the oceans. Even after he learned to fly, he did not get far above the surface of the earth, for the atmosphere soon becomes too rarefied to support the flight of planes. If you think of the earth as a large orange, man's flight in airplanes takes him about as high as the thickness of three or four sheets of paper. Travel by rockets into space is as different from "flying" as is an airplane from an outboard motorboat skimming above the water. The men who navigate our space ships will be a different breed than the pilots of airplanes. Mr. Wells tells you of the many new problems these future Astronauts will have to anticipate and solve in carrying out their strange new missions.

When the time comes that man can indeed climb into a space ship, take off and venture into outer space, he will have broken the bond which, from time immemorial, has tied him to Mother Earth. No longer is he bound to the surface of the earth. Now in the reaches of space, he can see the universe in its full spectrum and can personally explore the possibilities of life on other planets. Now he will have a new frontier and will have before him a new age of exploration and discovery to lend a ray of hope to the billions of people who soon will over-populate this earth on which we live.

Dr. John P. Hagen
National Aeronautics and Space Administration

ACKNOWLEDGMENTS

The National Aeronautics and Space Act became law in 1958, with most of the features recommended by the President of the United States. It gives our national objectives in exploring space and in developing space vehicles for this purpose.

"In due course a permanent manned satellite will be placed in orbit around the earth, to conduct research, and possibly as a station from which to organize deeper penetrations into space. As we master the required technology we will send an expedition to the moon, and later on to Mars, to Venus, and to more distant reaches of the solar system."

— Hugh L. Dryden, Deputy Administrator
National Aeronautics and Space Administration

Planning and building the equipment to carry out these objectives are members of American industry. Here are some leaders, to whom I am indebted for information and pictures which make this book about future events seem as though these already are "now." But so fast are we progressing, that some of these may indeed be "now" before much later.

Aerojet-General Corporation
American Bosch Arma
   Corporation
Bell Aircraft Corporation
Chance Vought Aircraft, Inc.
Convair (Astronautics)
   Division, General Dynamics
   Corporation
Douglas Aircraft Company, Inc.

Ford Motor Co., Aeronutronic
   Division
General Electric Company
Graflex, Inc.
Hughes Aircraft Company
International Business
   Machines
Kearfott Division, General
   Precision, Inc.

Lockheed Aircraft Corporation
The Martin Company
Melpar, Inc.
Minneapolis-Honeywell
   Regulator Company
NORAIR, division of Northrup
   Corporation
North American Aviation, Inc.
   and its Autonetics Division
Radiation, Inc.
Raytheon Company

Radio Corporation of America
Sperry Gyroscope Company
Westinghouse Electric
   Corporation

Also:

The Rand Corporation
Space Technology Laboratories,
   Inc., a subsidiary of
   Thompson Ramo Wooldridge,
   Inc.

I also wish to thank the Institute of Aerospace Sciences, The American Rocket Society, the National Aeronautics and Space Administration, and the U. S. Air Force and U. S. Navy.

— ROBERT WELLS

CREDITS FOR PHOTOGRAPHS

Aerojet-General Corporation, p. 21, 50, 54
American Bosch Arma Corporation,
   p. 12, 17, 20, 55, 63
Convair (Astronautics) Division, General
   Dynamics Corporation, p. 8, 46
Douglas Aircraft Company, Inc., p. 13
Ford Motor Co., Aeronutronic Division,
   p. 25, 64
General Electric Company, p. 58, 60, 62
Lockheed Aircraft Corporation, p. 15, 24,
   27, 29, 31
The Martin Company, p. 22, 53

Minneapolis-Honeywell Regulator
   Company, p. 42
National Aeronautics and Space
   Administration, p. 9, 14, 32, 33, 37,
   38, 39, 41, 44 (lower), 47, 48, 49,
   57, 59
NORAIR, division of Northrup
   Corporation, p. 18, 23, 51
U. S. Air Force, p. 1, 34, 35, 36, 40, 43,
   44 (upper)
U. S. Navy, p. 2, 11
Westinghouse Electric Corporation, p. 61

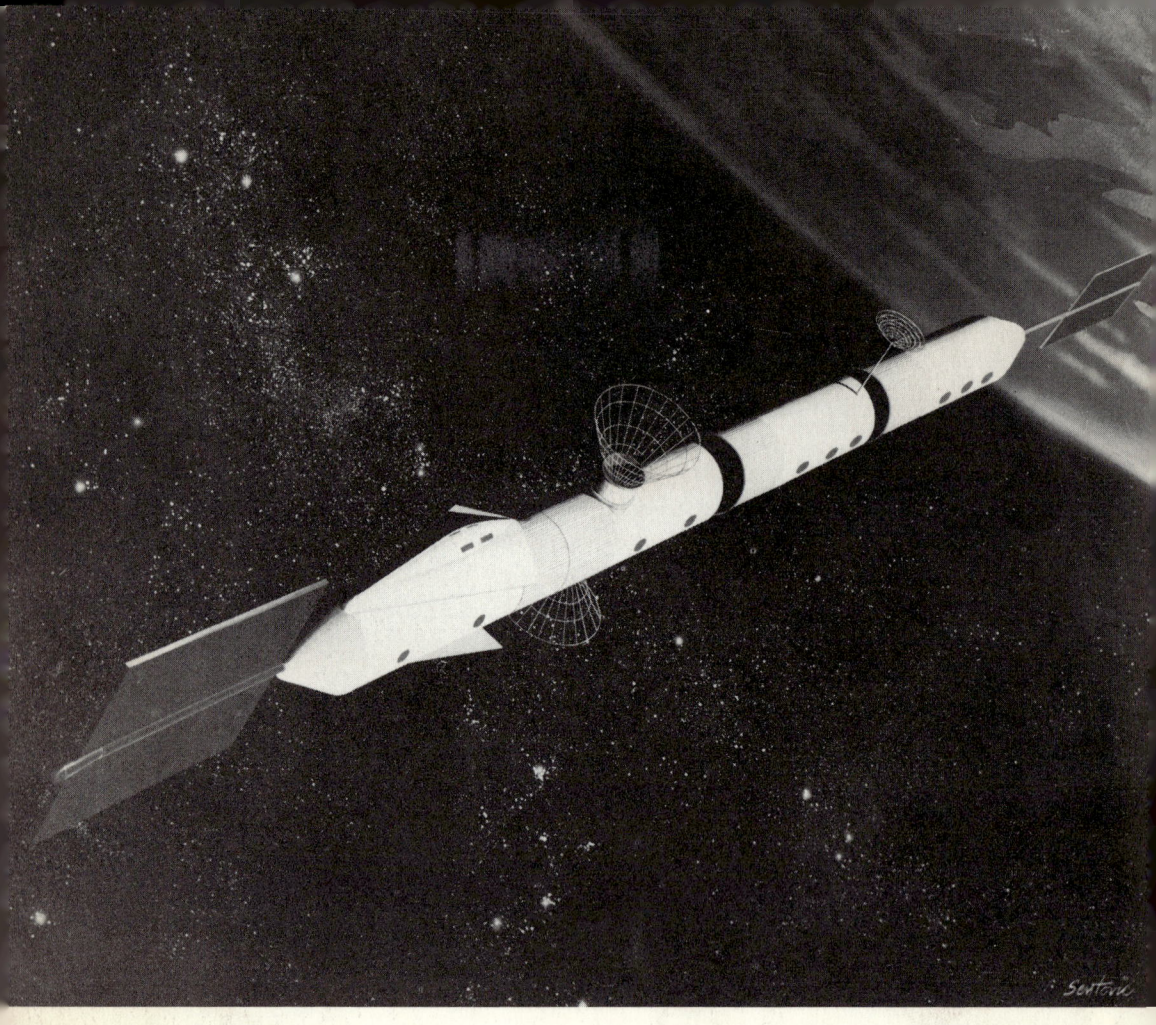

THE ASTRONAUT sees to it that his spacecraft does the job assigned to it. Its control system for oxygen and air pressure, its control system which keeps the craft "right-side up" in flight — and most of its other systems — can work automatically. They usually do. Yet the astronaut is in command of these systems and their controls.

He is the manager of all these systems. Each has instruments which are on the astronaut's control panel. He monitors these instruments — he watches them carefully — and sees that his spacecraft is working correctly.

If his instruments show that his craft is not on course or is not spaceworthy, he decides what to do — and does it. If he wishes, he can take control with his own hands and brain.

Facing him is his instrument and control console. In one kind of spacecraft, different groups of controls — handles and push-buttons — are painted a different color, so that the astronaut can quickly find the one he wants. His emergency controls are

painted red. Switches are made so that he can operate them easily when wearing his gloved pressure suit inflated.

A panel of instruments tells him by green lights that his vehicle's automatic operations — during lift-off and ascent and then while in orbit — are taking place, and in the right order. This is the sequence panel. If one item fails to work right, its name plate turns red. Then the astronaut may choose to work that control manually.

Other instruments tell the astronaut of his craft's acceleration and altitude; and flight instruments, its "attitude." A battery of clocks tells him not only the time, but also time-to-go until reaching target, time-from-launching — and just timers for any operation whose length he wishes to measure. Because this spacecraft travels so fast, things happen quickly; the astronaut, unlike the pilot of the slower airplane, is more interested in the *trend* — in what looks as if it will happen in the moments ahead — than in what is happening right *now*.

The environmental control panel's instruments show that his craft's atmosphere has enough oxygen, enough pressure, not too much moisture — among other things. More sections of controls are for his electrical system, his communications — and any special instruments his particular mission needs.

In fact, his spacecraft itself is designed to suit the kind of mission the astronaut is to accomplish with it. Perhaps his mission is to join his craft with another already in orbit — a space station — or to travel deep into space and circle another planet for observation.

Heavily-loaded atomic rocket spirals out free from earth. Destination: moon.

Above earth's atmosphere and spiraling out fast enough to counteract the pull of earth's gravity, his spacecraft travels through space like any other heavenly body. Its guidance and control must be by laws not of the straight-flight airplane but of the curved-flight stars.

If his mission is to join with a manned laboratory orbiting high above earth's atmosphere, his space vehicle must take up the space lab's orbit. And it must match its speed of orbiting. And finally, to join with it, the astronaut's craft must arrive there at the right time, too.

Travel at such great speeds and distances and changes in direction requires more and faster calculations than the astronaut can make alone. An electronic computer provides the information by which the astronaut guides his craft — or monitors it while it is automatically guided — close enough to its destination for the astronaut to operate it manually the last short distance to target.

Instrument panel of an orbiting astronomical laboratory

THREE-AXIS CONTROLLER

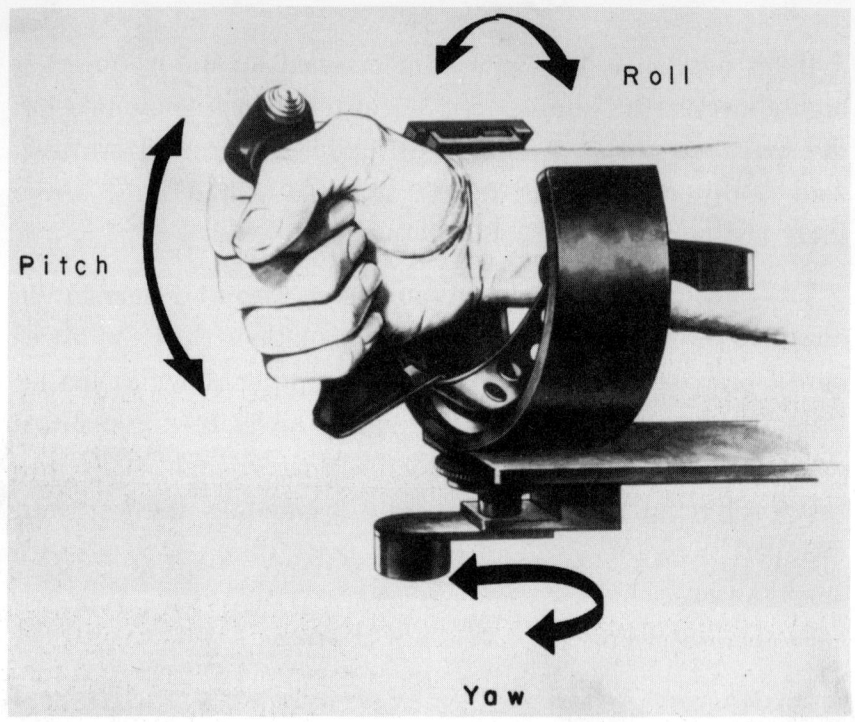

His vehicle's "attitude" is the direction it is facing, compared with the direction it is traveling. For in airless, weightless space, the spacecraft may be pointing one way, but traveling another. He adjusts its attitude by moving a short stick-like control which he holds in his right hand — the *three-axis attitude controller*. It has an axis for roll, one for pitch, one for yaw. He uses it to "trim" his craft. If he is close enough to earth, he can use earth's horizon as a "level" for his craft.

But unlike a plane with wings and ailerons, the astronaut's craft levels by small reaction jets and gyroscopes. Even though it may have stubby wings, these are of no use out here in space.

14

For there is no air here, no friction against his spacecraft — nor against any object. Not even against him. When he climbs, space-suited, *out* of his spacecraft while it is in flight — and there are times when he will do just that — he and his spacecraft just keep traveling, both at the same speed.

And because they do, they appear to be standing still — for

there is nothing to measure their speed against. Yet they are traveling at some five miles per *second*. There is no "up" — and no place to fall "down" to.

Two sets of doors — an airlock — safeguard his craft's supply of air as the astronaut climbs out of his craft to work in space. Perhaps he is to repair his spacecraft, or to assemble a space station from parts earlier rocketed up from earth where they were made. He needs oxygen and air pressure, just as he did within the spacecraft. His space suit provides these.

But now, how does he get about to do his work, floating freely in space, traveling some 18,000 miles an hour — or faster — while seeming to stand still? And how can he be stopped from an endless spin or tumble in this airless, frictionless place?

Here again his space suit fills his need — with a built-in jet propulsion system which he controls by push buttons in a control box mounted on his suit's chest. Now he maneuvers himself as if *he* were a spacecraft: these buttons control the roll, pitch and yaw — of himself; and other buttons control his velocity and change in direction — very accurately, for a vehicle or a man in a spin will continue to spin, without stopping, unless stopped by some outside force.

For moving to or from his ship, he uses controls which operate his own built-in reaction jet. Although its thrust is only a few pounds, it's enough.

Perhaps he is to help assemble the parts of a space station. These have been delivered from earth by rockets which put

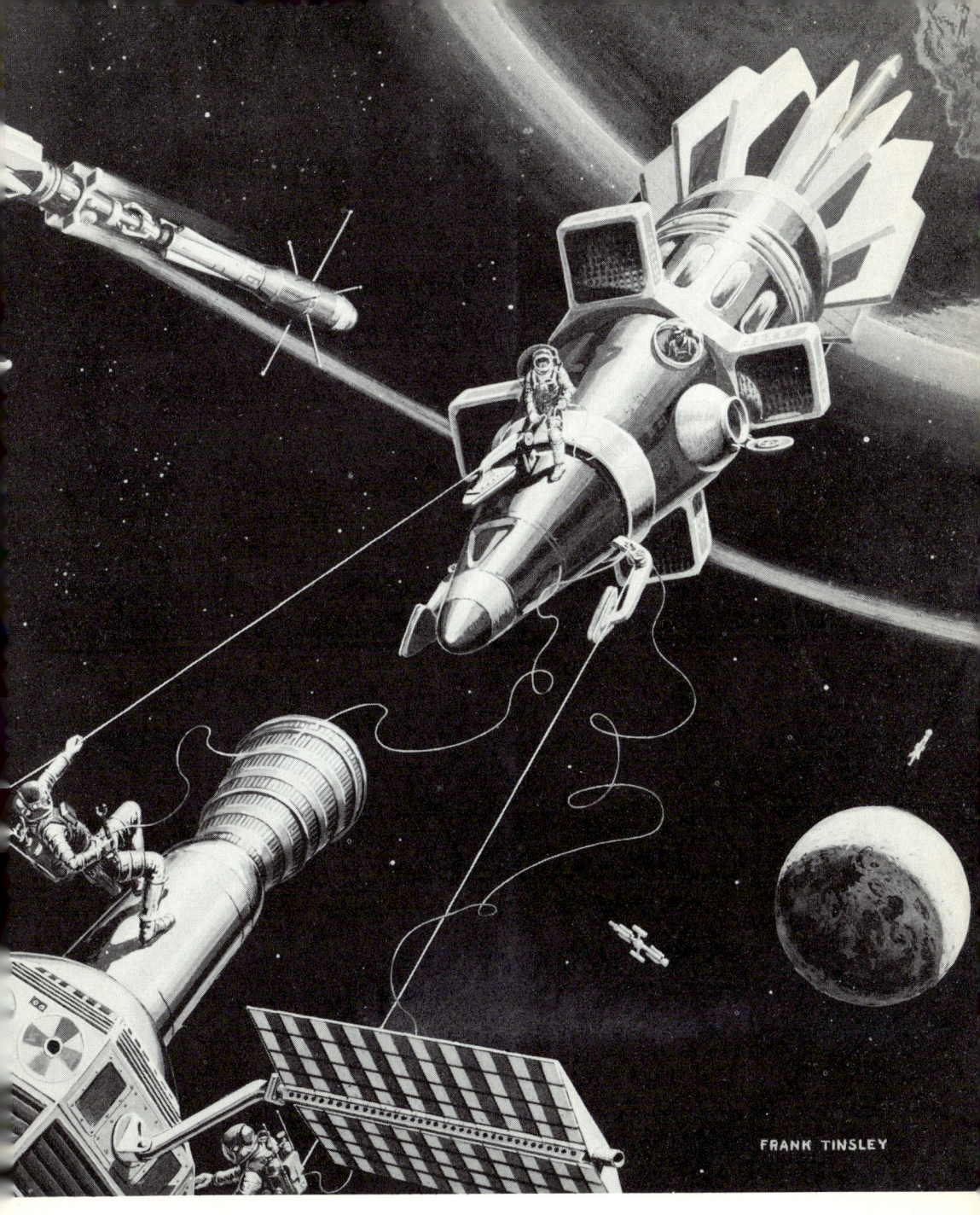

Crewmen attach their space tug to a worn-out unmanned satellite before sending it speeding into earth's atmosphere for vaporization.

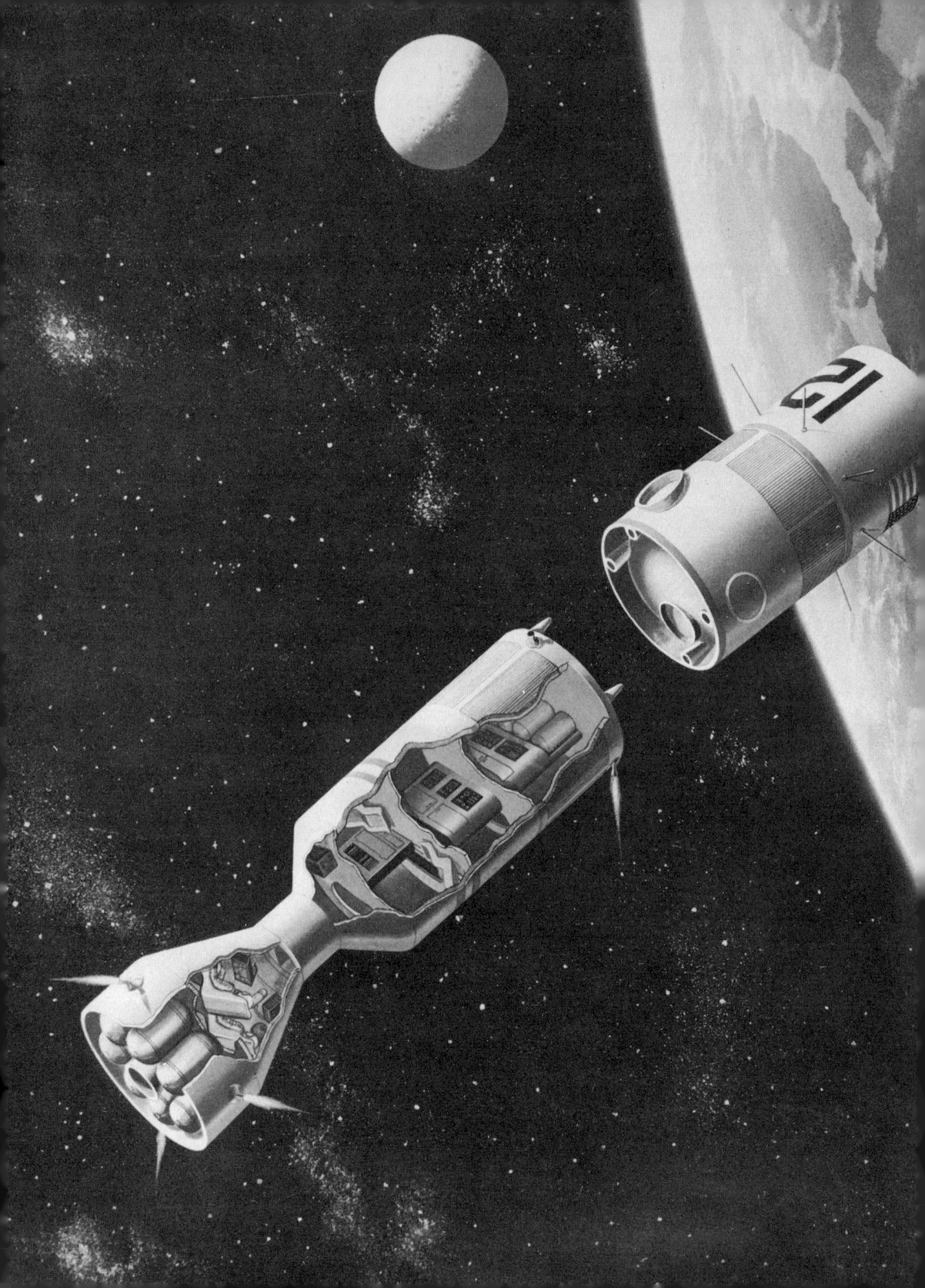

them in orbit, all fairly close together. Now these men in space work to fasten these parts together, to build a space station too huge to send up in one piece. Or perhaps their job is to locate an instrumented unmanned satellite which is not working properly, and either repair it or get it out of the way by destroying it. Whatever the job, these men in their space suits can move about in space — outside their craft — by spurts of power, thrust, from the reaction jets built into their space suits.

Similar propulsion controls are built into a special kind of space suit, too — really more a miniature spacecraft — that the astronaut uses for working in space. It is big enough just for him. He is completely enclosed in it. This suit is rigid, shaped like a Coke bottle. From it protrude several arms. Each holds a different kind of tool. Inside the suit, he works manipulators which control these arms and tools. Outside, the arms move their tools, just as he is directing them to do.

To do his work in this special suit, he must be able to maneuver himself around. Also, he must be able to adjust his "attitude." He does this by a joy stick which he uses something like the three-axis attitude controller in the spacecraft.

Some astronauts may use another kind of reaction jet device which looks something like a miniature rocket guided by handle bars mounted on a single column. The man holds this device before him. If he wishes to go "right," he turns it to the right — and it pulls him along after it, in the direction it faces.

Assembly in space of a three-part satellite. The maneuverable two-man capsule has joined the life-support section and maneuvers to couple with the space laboratory.

Passing one of Saturn's moons, the spacecraft's crew detaches their ferry-rocket from its mile-across solar-radiation propelled sail.

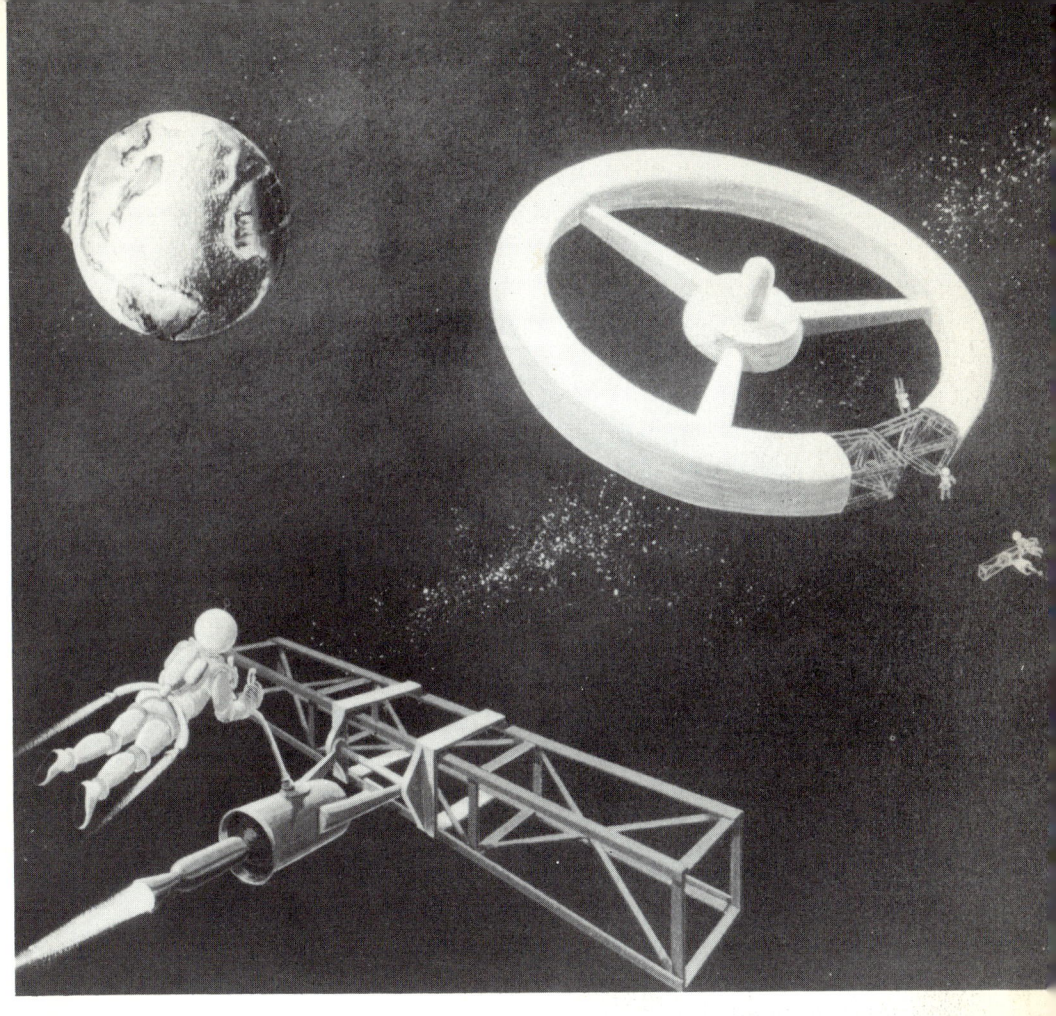

A one-man rocket propulsion device moves man and cargo.

   These jet propulsion devices work like the big rocket engines of spacecraft do — by thrust. Out through the exhaust, at the back of the engine, shoot white-hot gases from the big rocket engines or compressed air from the space suit jet propulsion devices. Other kinds of fuels may be used — but the principle of all is the same: action, and re-action. The action — the force

21

INFLATABLE STRUCTURED SPACE VEHICLE

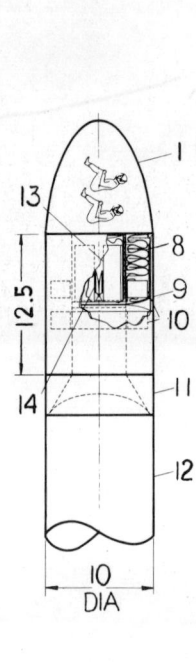
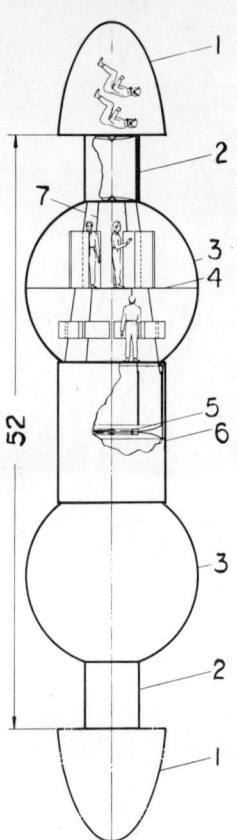

LEGEND

1 - ESCAPE AND RESUPPLY VEHICLE
2 - AIRLOCK
3 - 16 FT DIAMETER INFLATABLE SPHERE
4 - STOWABLE LIGHTWEIGHT COMPARTMENTIZER
5 - PRESSURE BULKHEAD
6 - MIDDLE BAY
7 - MAIN RIGGING CABLES - EQUIPMENT DEPLOYMENT
8 - STOWED INFLATABLE SPHERE
9 - CONTAINER SECTION
10 - STOWED ANNULAR EQUIPMENT
11 - BOOSTER ADAPTER
12 - BOOSTER
13 - AIRLOCK STOWED EQUIPMENT
14 - RETRACTED AIRLOCK HATCH

The pilot of an outbound spacecraft noses his craft to a space fueling station to take on liquid air.

— of the blast coming out the exhaust is matched by a re-action of force going in the opposite direction. Face the jet exhaust down, and the space vehicle goes up from the launching pad. Direct the exhaust of the space suit to the left, and the man in space goes to the right. Blast harder, go faster.

Thrust nozzles, and control actuators to direct them, propel still another kind of manned work vehicle in space. Like the rigid space suit, this vehicle also has arms protruding from it; within it, astronauts control their manipulators that make those arms work. But this vehicle is large enough for more than one man alone. Some carry two men, some carry an even larger crew: their job, to use this craft as a kind of space "tugboat," to round up the components — segments — of a space station

23

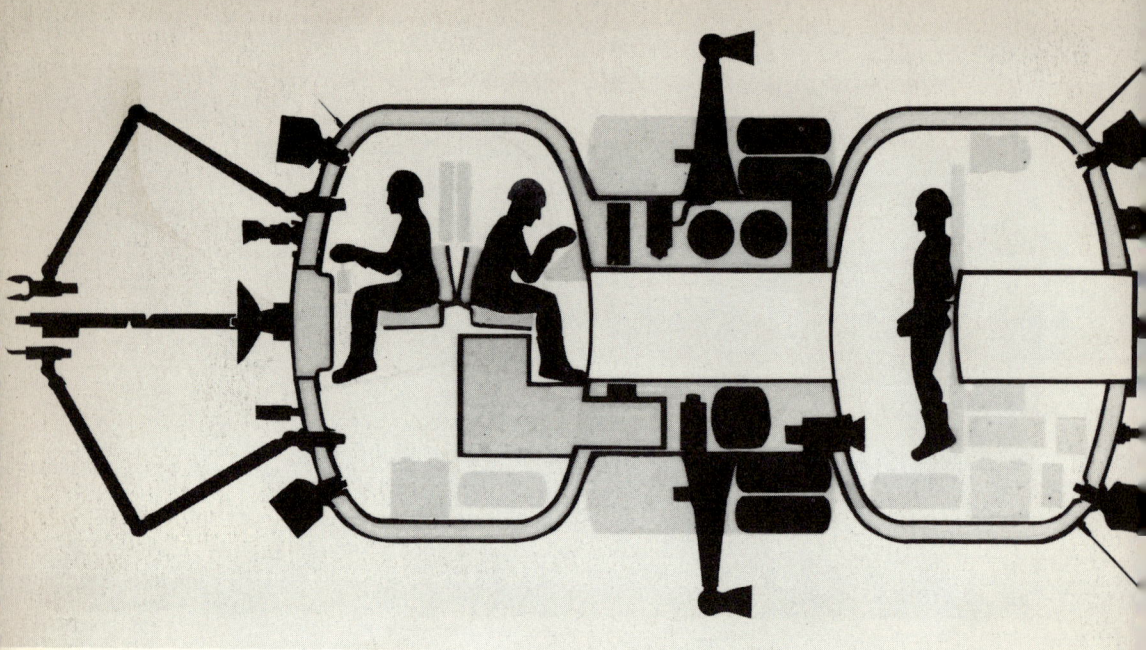

Cross-section showing inside of astrotug

from where rockets had placed them in orbit. When the astronauts have brought these to one place — dragged there by this vehicle — they then fit the parts together and build a space station. And they use the space tugboat — the *astrotug*, as some call it — to do this job.

The tug's radar searches and then finds the components for the space station-to-be, circling in orbit. These may be a great distance away. The radar identifies them as the "target" before the astronauts direct their tug all the way there. The radar also tells the tug's computer how far away these targets are, and in which direction. Then the tug's space-pilot starts the tug on its way to round up these space station parts. He initiates the capture mission.

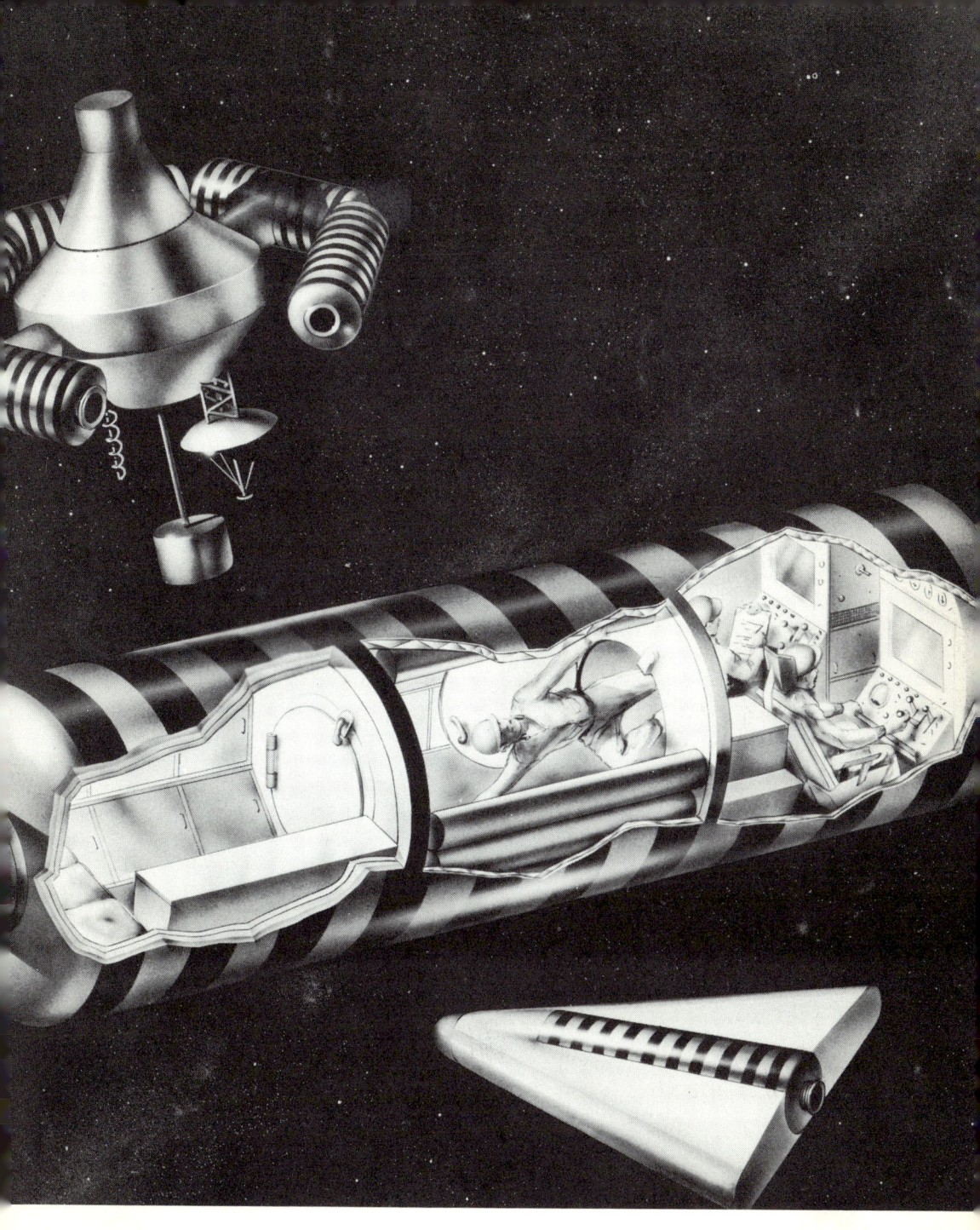

In weightless space flight, component of space station approaches its destination. Winged component prepares for re-entry into earth's atmosphere.

Automatically, its course computed and corrected by the computer, the tug moves into the target's orbit and at the proper speed to take it to within only 100 yards or so of that target.

Now the astronaut cuts out the automatic controls and takes the vehicle's operation into his own hands. At his console of instruments and controls, he "flies" his astrotug at a speed of only a few feet per second more — or less, if his target is in back of him — from the target's orbiting speed. The distance between the two slowly but surely closes. He is very careful — damage to the target might make it useless; damage to his own vehicle might destroy it, with him in it. Now his craft barely inches along — compared to the target's speed — and then tug and target make contact.

At the operator's console within the astrotug are controls for the manipulators, the arms, outside the vehicle. The "hands" of these arms are toolheads — wrenches, clamps, and the like. On the console are exact miniatures of these manipulators. Each is connected to the big one it resembles. As the operator moves the miniature, the large one moves in just the same way. He watches through his viewing port — or on the screen of his closed-circuit TV. Without leaving the comfort of his vehicle — with its air and food and livable pressure — the operator manipulates the arms and hands to take careful but firm hold on the component that is to be part of the space station.

Now back on automatic control, the tug tows the component according to the instructions long ago programmed into its computer. The astronaut, who serves as pilot, monitors the instru-

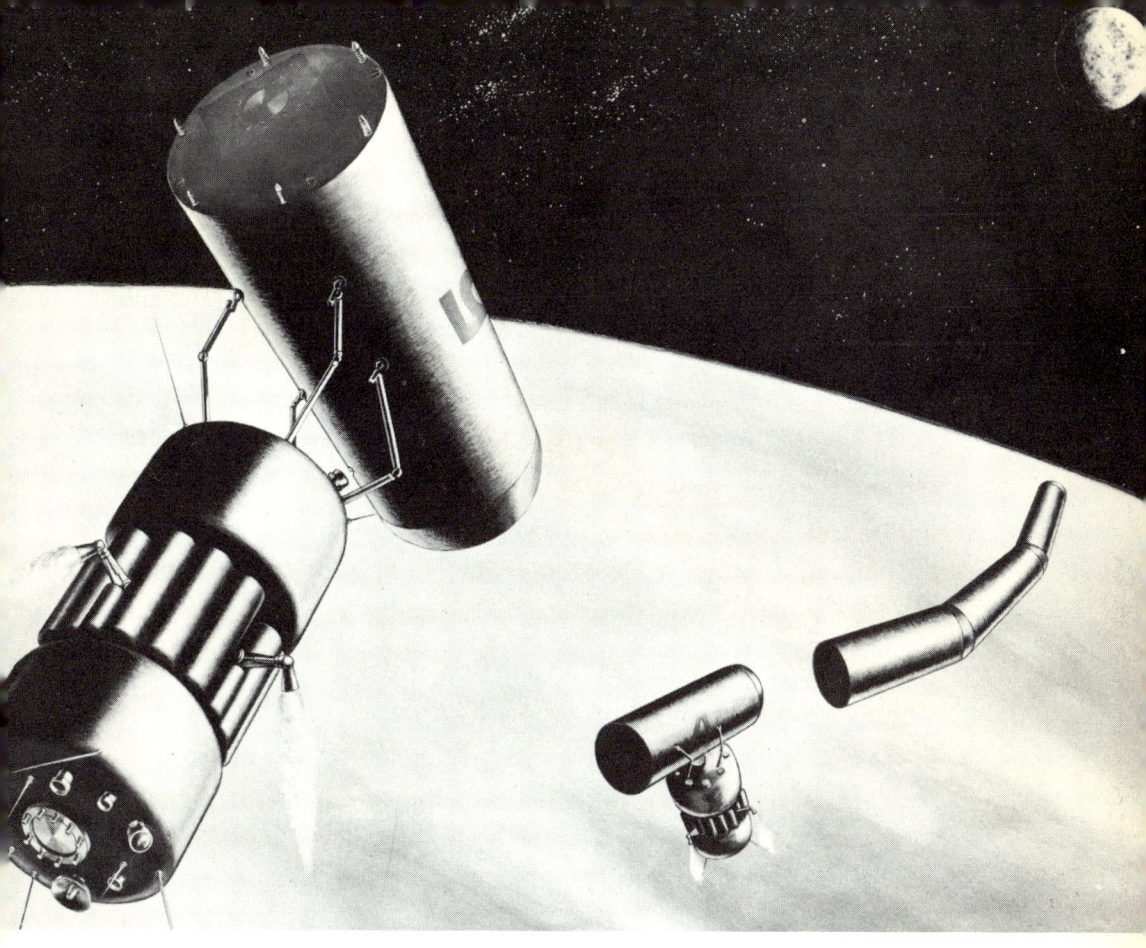

The tug's tool-head arms take hold of space station component.

ments on his control panel. He makes sure his craft delivers the component — a big tube — to the assembly area. Once again, he takes over manual control of his vehicle, and maneuvers the tube to just the right spot for joining with the others already gathered there.

Then the tug moves off on another capture mission. By the time it returns, the components brought together earlier are at the same temperature.

Now they can be joined precisely. The operator at the console of miniature manipulators lines up these components, brings them together and then fastens them firmly. Space crews in other tugs are doing the same kind of job; often they work together, completing the space station.

When all the segments of the space station are joined together, the space-pilot of the tug fastens his craft to the now completed space station. Airlock of tug joins airlock of space station. Now the crew transfers from tug to station; now begins the job of completing the station's interior.

They filled the station with air first, from a supply tank put into orbit from earth, to provide a livable pressure within. Now they remove the temporary walls which sealed the ends of the big tubes, and connect the wires and pipes which run through each one. When the tube was lofted into orbit, it carried its own equipment — fastened down tightly. Now the men unfasten it, put it in place. They put the mechanical and electrical equipment in working order. A week after the components were rocketed into orbit, there is a complete space station ready for its crew. The tugs, also put into orbit by rocket, remain there, too. They will work with other craft which may be within range of this space staion. These little "workhorses" do not return to earth at all.

But their crews can — via the space commuter which brought them up there, then returned to earth, and now brings the space station's crew. These commuter vehicles also will keep the space station supplied with food, water, equipment, supplies.

Since these shuttle vehicles have a quite different sort of job, they are built and operated differently from the tugs. For one thing, they must return to earth; so they have some sort of wings which allow the pilot-astronaut to glide them to a landing. He flies them like an airplane, once they have returned from space to where there is enough air to give some lift to their wings. But they must be spacecraft, too, to be able to go again into space and be maneuvered there by reaction jets.

Leaving earth in a space commuter, astronaut and passengers are fastened in to their form-molded couches for rocket blast-off and ascent into space. While they are pinned down by gravity forces now, the vehicle flies on automatic control.

Multi-stage rocket, before lofting and orbiting a commuter vehicle.

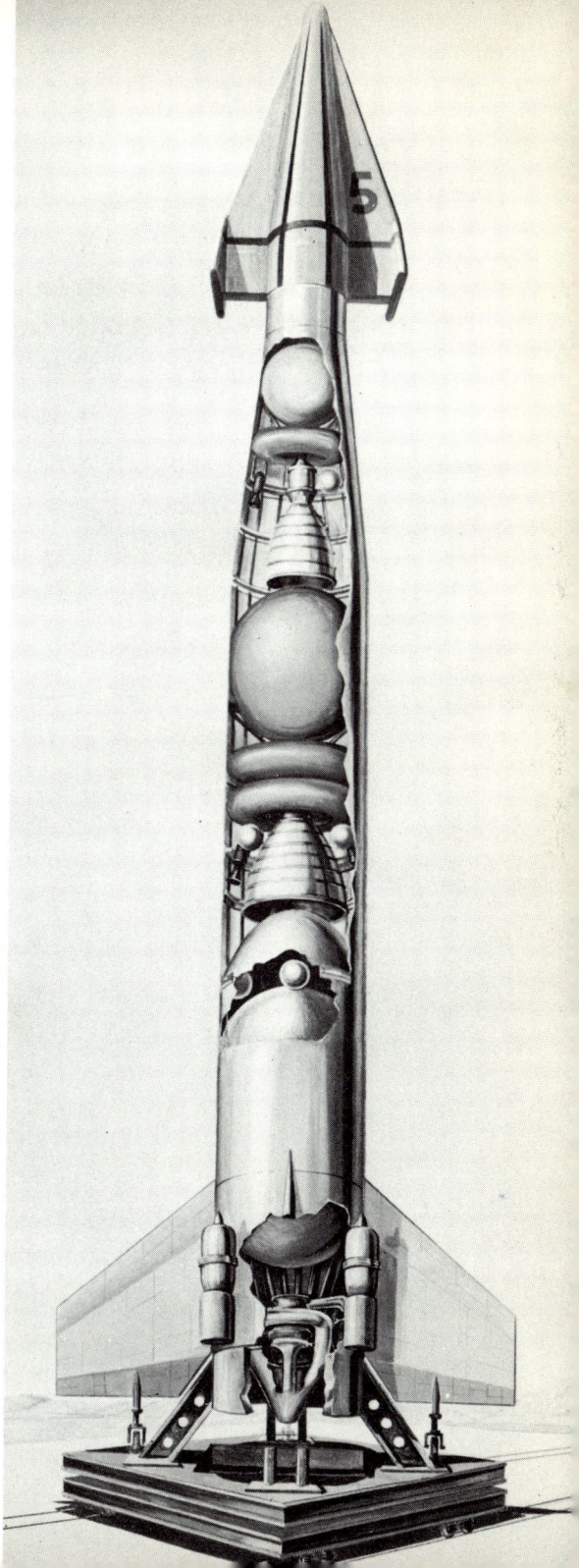

The exhausted lower stages drop away — if nuclear-powered, these stages may be able to glide back to earth and be used again. And what would be the last stage of a rocket — this time the stubby-winged craft with astronaut and passengers inside — goes into orbit. Once in orbit, g-forces give way. The astronaut monitors the controls. His craft follows its computer's programmed orders and maneuvers into the orbit of their target.

Close to target — the space station — the astronaut guides this space-ferry the remaining short distance. He uses reaction jets, as did the astronaut in the tug. And he performs this closure maneuver carefully, too — until airlock of commuter is joined to airlock of station.

On a trip back to earth — perhaps to return the tug astronauts, perhaps to change space station crews — the astronaut who pilots the space commuter now must cope with probably the most dangerous part of the entire round-trip — re-entry into earth's atmosphere. For if his vehicle's nose points too directly to earth, the craft will travel too fast. Then friction with air as it enters earth's atmosphere will create great heat — enough to melt the ship's metal skin in only a few seconds.

Automatic controls help the astronaut. Sensors measure the craft's speed and temperature — and command the controls to adjust the craft's course up again, out of atmosphere and friction and heat, if they sense overheating. Buffeted by forces created by his spacecraft's speed and the resistance it meets in the lower, heavier atmosphere, the astronaut monitors his instruments and prepares to take over manually if the automatic controls fail.

A three-stage rocket boosts the spacecraft (1) and (2) until it reaches orbit altitude (3) where its pilot guides it to target (4).

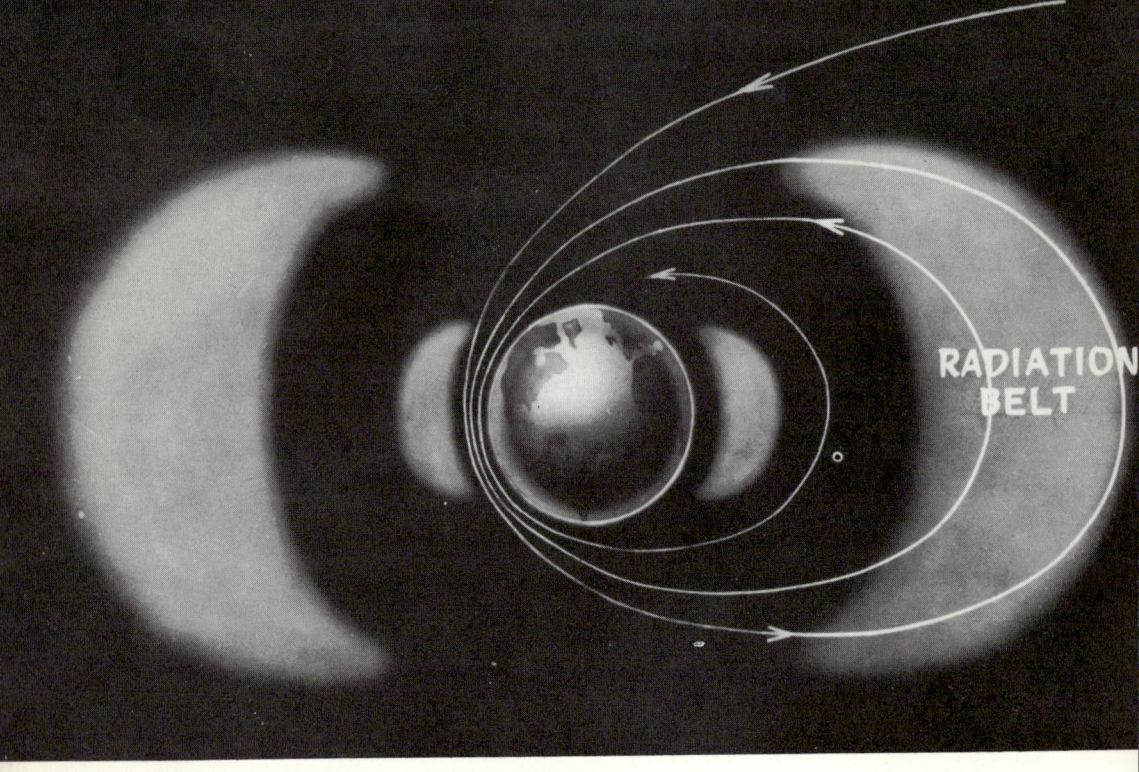

The returning spacecraft makes several passes through earth's atmosphere, each ellipse braking its speed more and avoiding the Great Radiation Belts as much as possible.

But they don't fail. The space pilot can see that they are guiding him and his craft at just the right angle which brings his ship into the atmosphere, slowing it without burning it up. The heat gauge on his instrument panel shows green — not the yellow for "caution" nor the red for "danger."

His craft decelerates from hypersonic to supersonic speed. Now he adjusts its course just slightly, so that he can land right on base — and not half a continent away.

Buffeted — yet slowed — by the still heavier atmosphere, the craft registers its speed on its instruments. The astronaut now reads "subsonic speed." Now his craft handles more like airplane than spacecraft. Now the stubby wings slice through air thick enough to give them lift. Now his airplane-type controls gain response when he moves them. He turns a switch, and his turbojets ignite and flame into life — with a welcome roar, so different from the silence of space.

He flies by instrument; and as he guides his ship closer to base, he sees two pips in his radar scope. Two needle-nosed jet interceptors are speeding to meet and escort him to a landing. Soon these blips are the airplanes themselves. They take station on either side of the astronaut's craft coming in from space, and guide it to base, then over the runway, and touchdown.

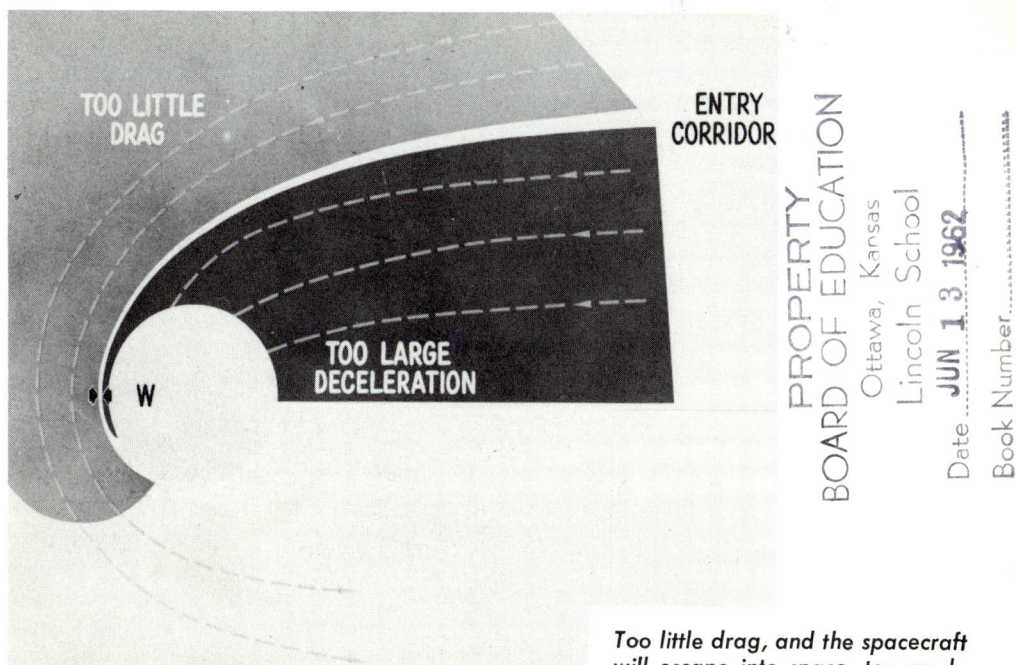

Too little drag, and the spacecraft will escape into space; too much, and it will overheat and burn.

This powered, gliding commuter craft that brings the astronaut safely back to earth developed from earlier ones — the Air Force X-15, designed with Navy and NASA help, for one. Speed above 3,000 miles an hour; altitude, 100 miles — space indeed — and encountering temperatures from $-300°F$ to a re-entry heat of $1200°F$.

At these altitudes and speeds, this X-15's pilot is virtually an astronaut as he works, pressure-suited and air-cooled in his cockpit, monitoring his instruments. On the console, to the left, he operates the ballistic attitude control "stick" which fires jet thrusts on his ship's nose for pitch and yaw; and on wing tips, for roll. Here, too, is the powerplant throttle, and the eight toggle switches to fire the barrels for thrust. On the right are his communication switches and navigational aids.

In early test flights, the pilot himself was an instrument: attached to his body and space suit, small instruments learned and reported his physical condition. His ship radioed that information to monitors on the ground below, to tell them that the way to space was opening wider.

Later, came Dyna-Soar — 18,000 mile-an-hour powered glider, thrust into space by rocket. Its space pilot glides it around earth, dips it gently into the thickening atmosphere, controls it by its elevons and drag rudders to an airplane-like landing.

From these ships — and from their men — came the information which went into the design of this space commuter. It works well and safely — and its astronaut survives buffeting and heating.

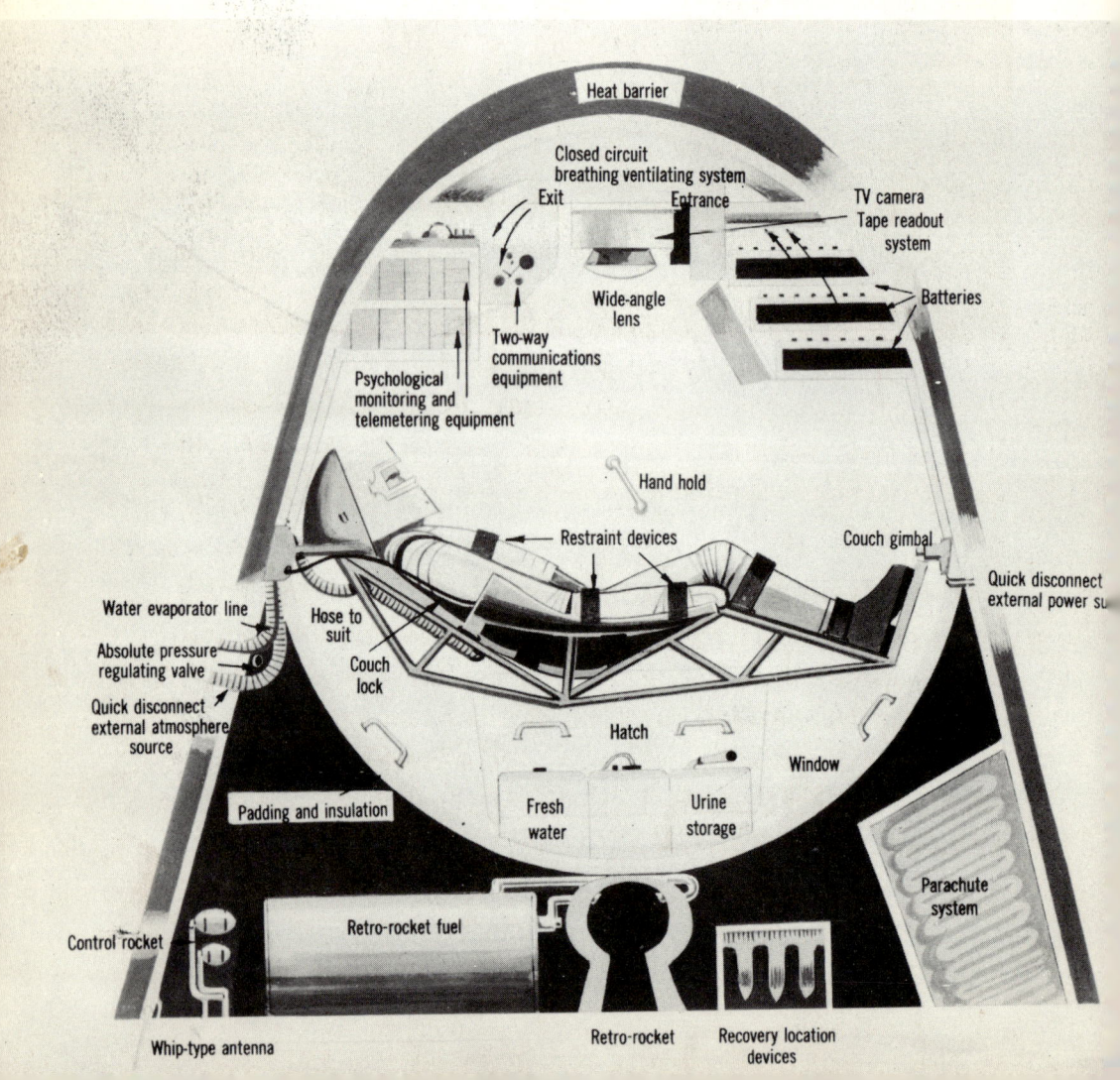

Training, while the astronaut was learning his work, also helps make sure he can do his job well. A large part of his training time is spent in the classroom, studying ballistics and trajectories, guidance and fuels, astronomy, geography. He learns how to make scientific observations — especially since he will have to monitor scientific instruments, too, in some of the early space flights.

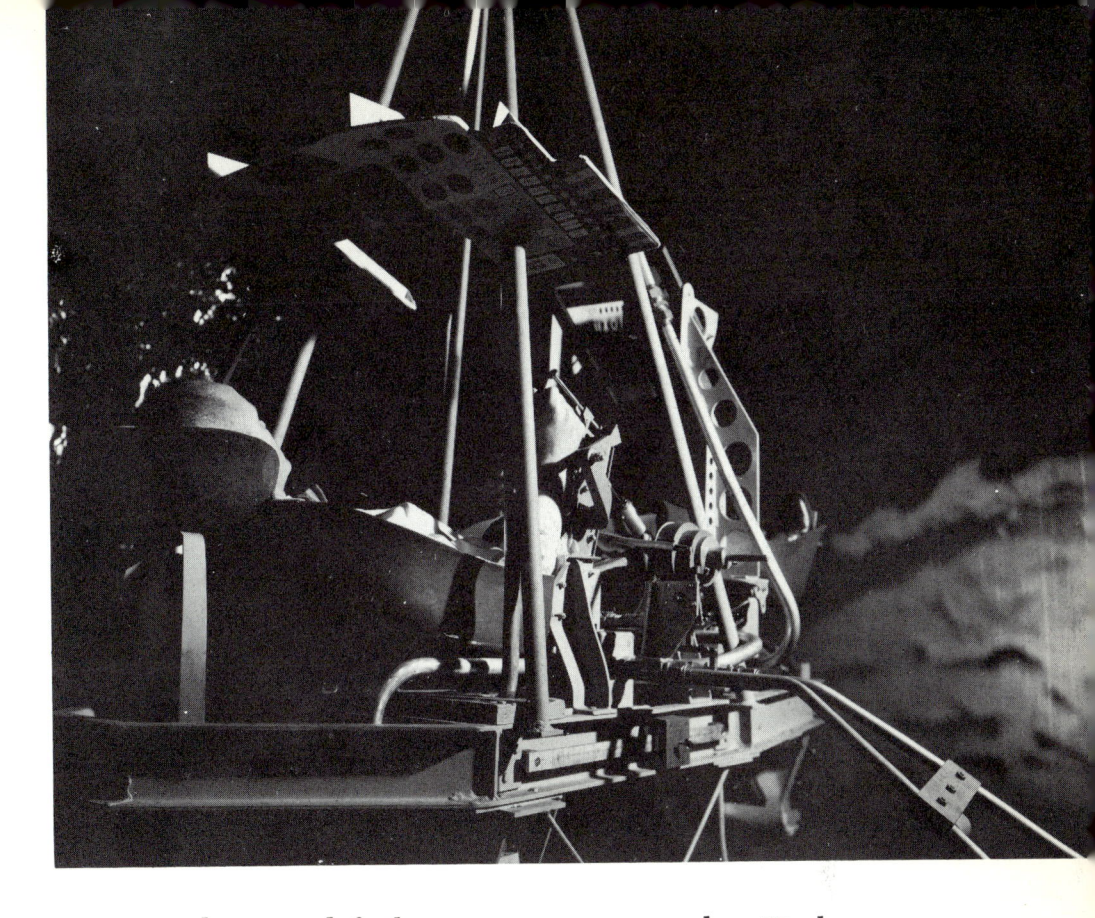

Another part of training is with "simulators" — devices which behave as his space vehicle will. In one of these, he learns how to operate the side-arm controller for his vehicle's attitude. The simulator moves in the same directions he moves his control, just as his space ship will move. And special motion pictures while he is doing this show him what he can expect to see when he later is in actual flight.

Another simulator — one which whirls him faster and faster — lets him learn the feel of those powerful gravity-forces, g-forces, which astronauts feel when their space vehicle hurtles up faster and faster through the atmosphere.

Now his training in this simulator grows more difficult. In front of him is a display — instruments and controls he will be monitoring and operating in space flight. Now he learns how to read his instruments accurately and to operate his controls carefully, even though his body is straining against the strong pull

38

of g-forces and his vision grows blurred. Suddenly, the instruments read, "Danger" — his instructor did that! — and the simulator responds to the way he operates the controls, and shows how well he will act in an emergency.

Still more training — this time, he learns about *the* vehicle he hopes to pilot: what are its systems and subsystems, how do these work and what do they do? And he learns, too, about the duties of the launch crew — the men who will start his space vehicle, with him strapped in it, on its flight into space.

And he learns something about the equipment they use, for his life will depend in part on these, too. In fact, he depends on many people who have planned and built and tested his vehicle and its many systems. And they depend on him to make good use of this work they have done for him.

There is special aviation flight training for these future astronauts whose space flights will take them hurtling back into earth's atmosphere: their stubby-winged craft will handle like airplanes once they have returned deeply enough into earth's atmosphere — or the atmosphere of another planet.

Teamwork makes the X-15 fly.

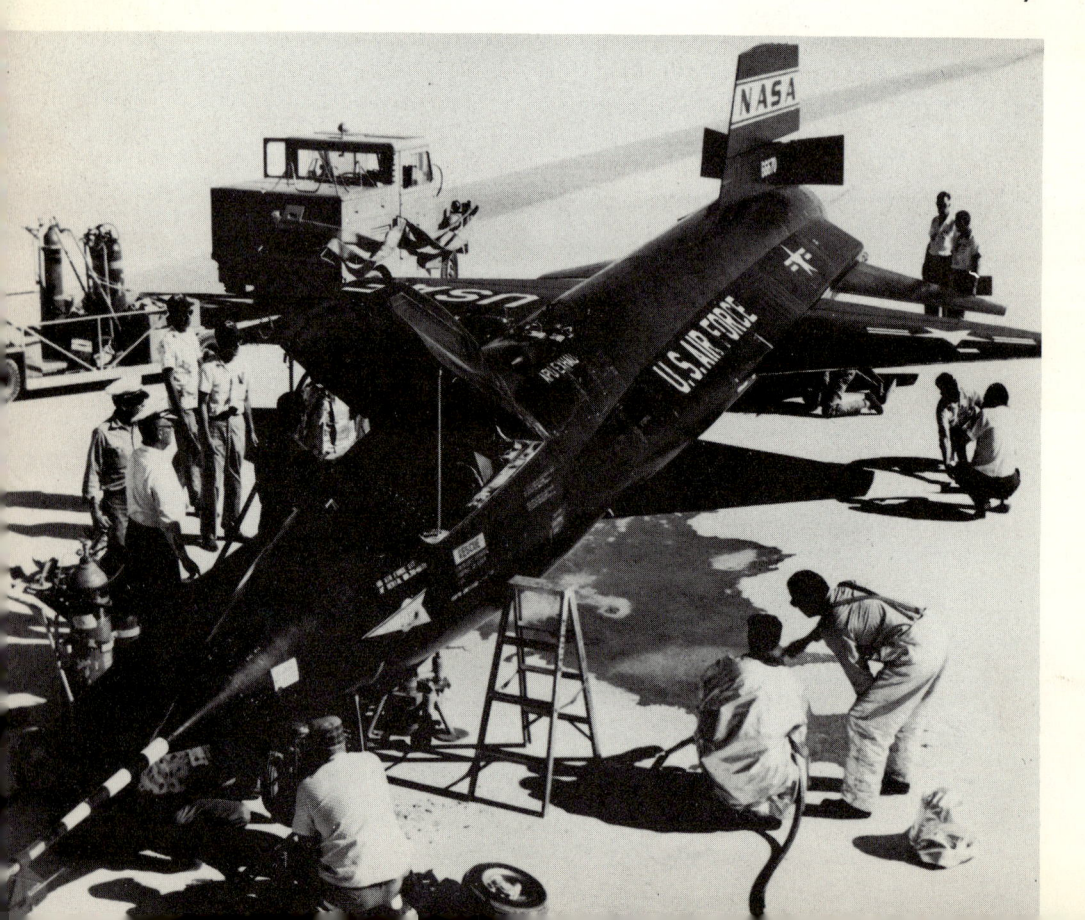

But what of the astronaut, coming back to earth in his spacecraft which travels so fast that it can circle our world in an hour-and-a-half, who overshoots his mark or is forced down in another part of the world? What if he lands in the middle of a desert, or in the sea? Does he know how to stay alive until help comes? His training includes these, too.

41

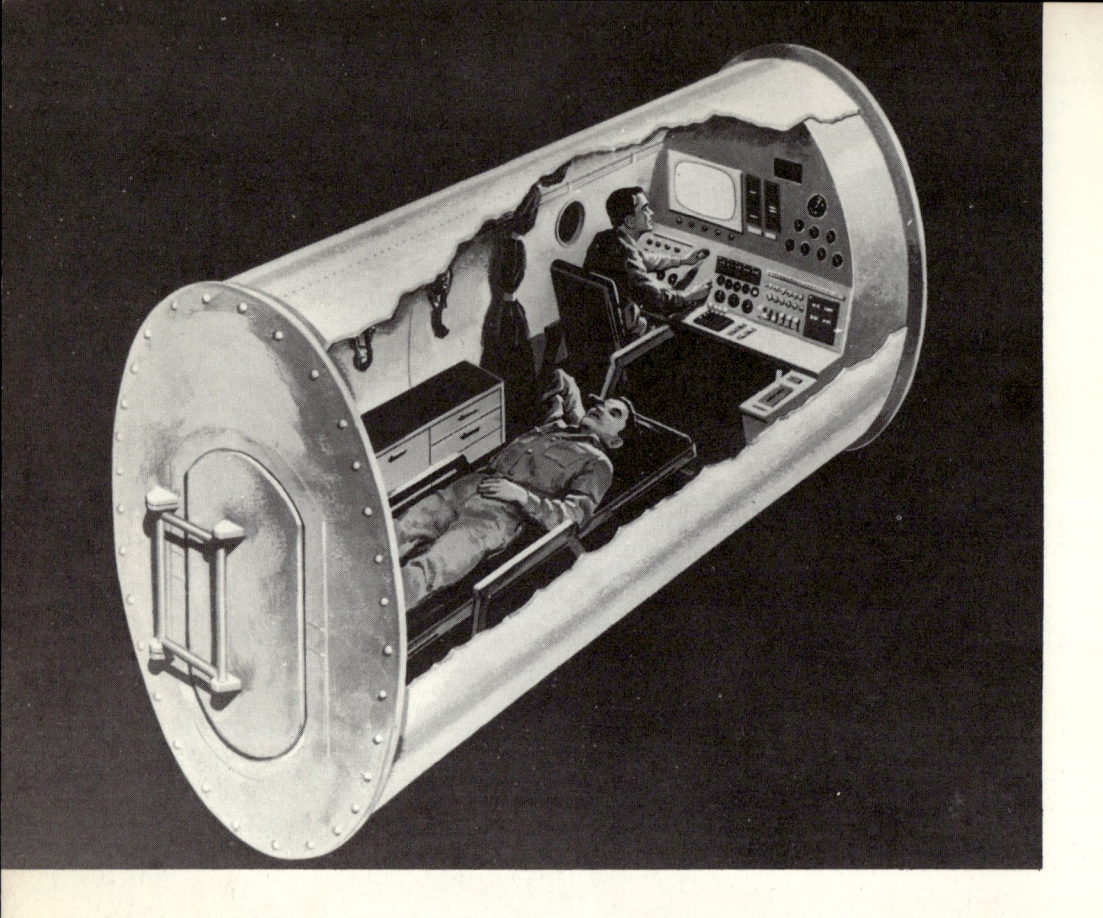

Still another kind of simulator does not move at all. But the astronauts in training can almost believe they are on a long space flight. This simulator is the copy of a spacecraft's cabin, complete with control panel. In this all-steel room, two astronauts spend a month living and working just as they would do on a space flight.

Aboard is their food, water and air. Locked in, they see no one but each other — for a month. As in space flight, they talk into a radio microphone for communication with the outside world. Although their "space ship" never leaves the ground, it seems to them as if they are indeed in space.

But one kind of space flight condition just cannot be simulated on the ground — zero-g. This is the opposite of the g-forces which strain at the astronaut when his vehicle is gaining or losing speed rapidly. Once his vehicle is in orbit — once its "outward" speed is fast enough to balance the pull of gravity — the astronaut feels no pull at all of gravity. He floats within his craft — as do all objects not fastened down. This strange thing also happens when he is outside his spacecraft, too. To learn how zero-g feels, and how to monitor instruments and work controls while weightless — for that is the feel of zero-g — the astronaut must take this part of his training in a speeding plane flying a planned arc.

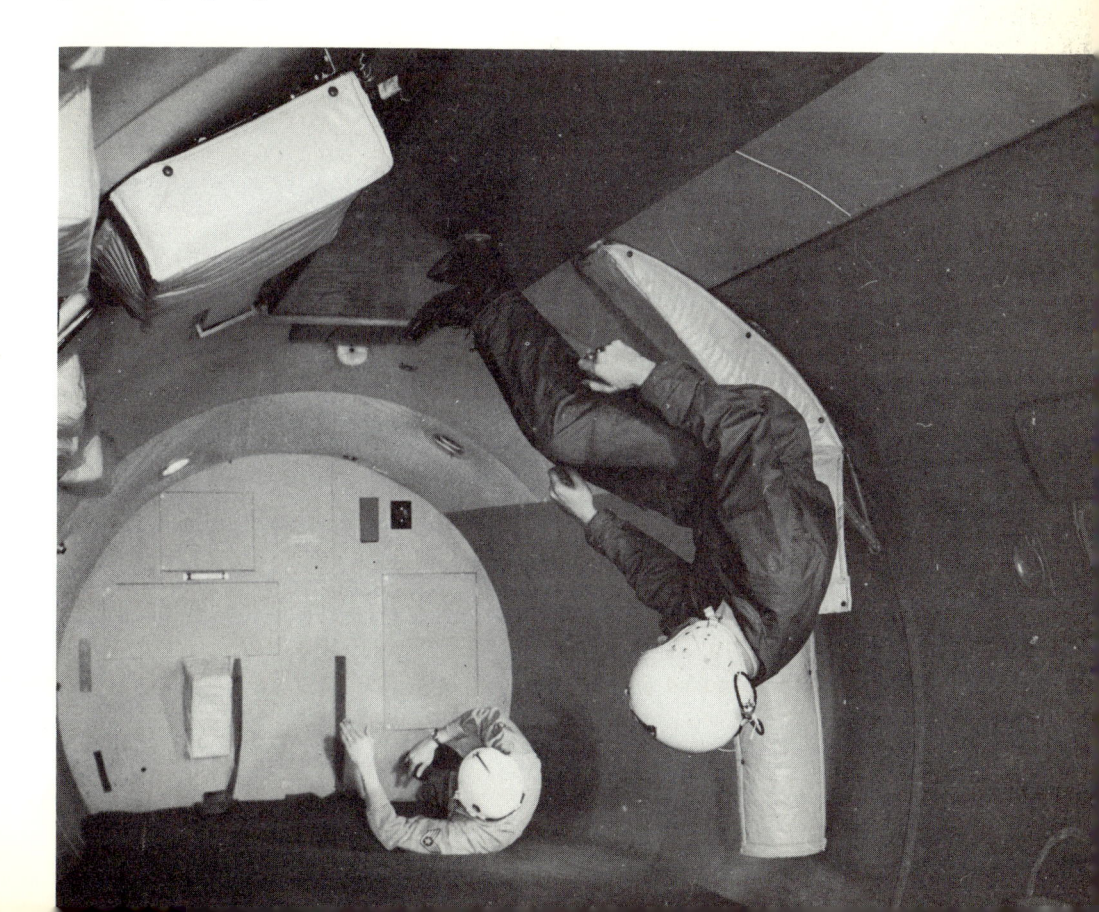

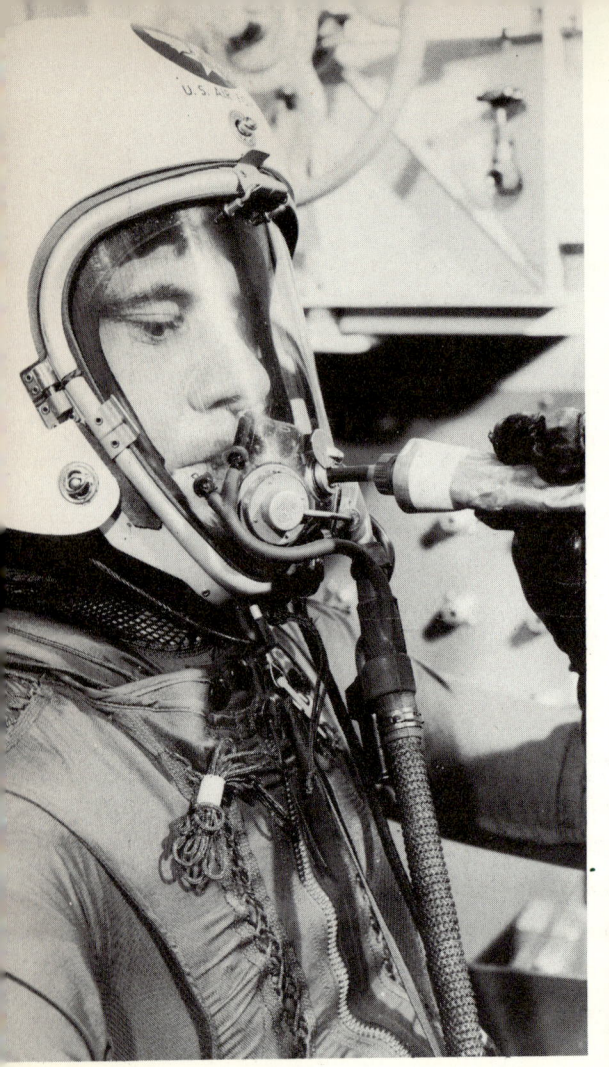

Squeeze-tube for feeding in weightlessness

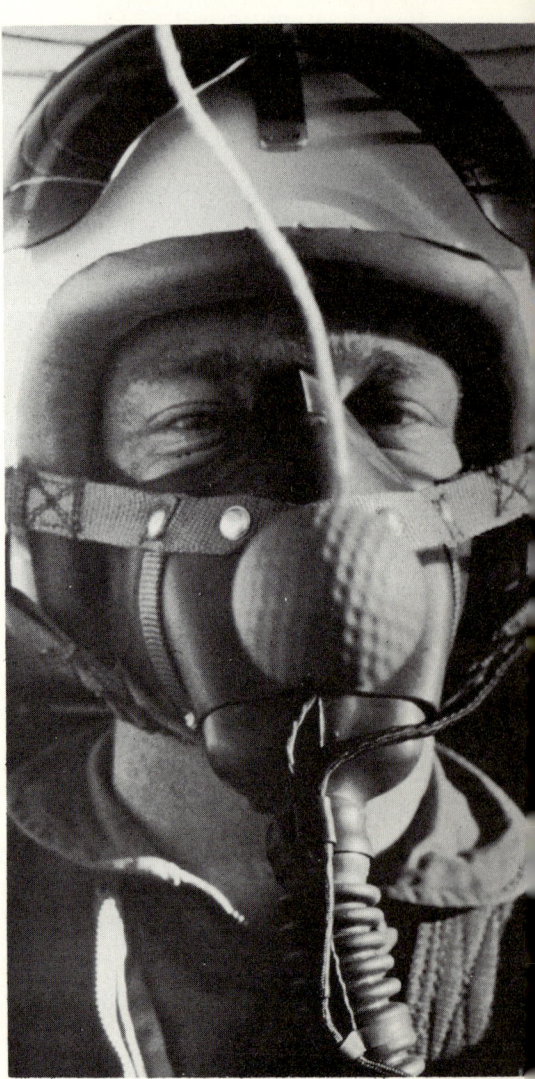

In weightlessness, the string on a suspended golf ball grows slack.

Weightlessness is one of the trade-marks of space flight. It can play tricks on a man's ability to see correctly, or to move his hands in just the way he wants them to go — until he learns how. And the astronaut must learn. In space flight, he must be alert and capable. His vehicle's immense speed magnifies small errors into big ones. And to correct errors may use up fuel — precious fuel not easily spared from the supply he needs for return to earth from, perhaps, a strange world. And that's also one reason why accurate navigation is so important to the astronaut.

His course was programmed in to his vehicle's computer, after being very carefully calculated, long before the flight started. The automatic navigational system checks itself; star sensors and sun seekers and other navigational aids check the positions of the spacecraft with the positions of the stars by which it is being navigated. The computer compares this information with what it "remembers" this information should be. Then it computes any changes in course and sends these, in electrical pulses, to the motors which control the jets. These blast — only a very little, but just enough to nudge the vehicle back exactly on course.

The astronaut can switch out these automatic operations, and control this navigating himself. But a computer can do this complicated navigating better than can a man. Still, when his vehicle at last brings him close to a distant target, he may have to make final adjustments.

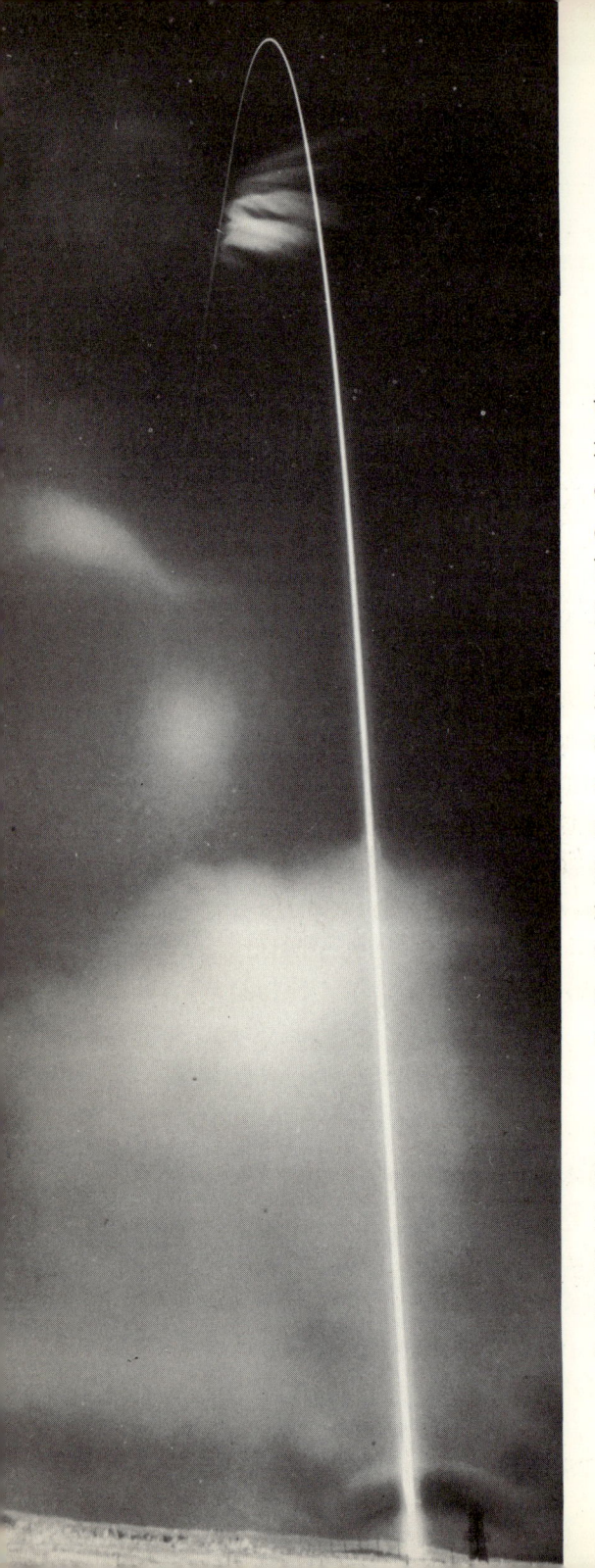

If his craft now is coasting through space, after lofting by rocket, it is traveling in a long curve, rather than in an easily computed straight line. Heavenly bodies travel in elliptical orbits. Because of these curves, an astronaut's flight to the moon, around it, and back to earth, may be about one million miles long — even though the moon is only about one-quarter of that distance away. And navigating to a moving target — a space station traveling at some five miles per second — is a very precise piece of work.

The kind of navigation the astronaut does depends upon the kind of mission he is on. Is it to land on another planet, and then return? Or to find and pull alongside a disabled weather satellite only three hundred miles out?

Or is he to guide a supply vehicle to an orbiting space station, and attach his vehicle to it? The answer will tell him what his navigation must be. And it also tells him how to proceed when he gets to target, and how he will maneuver his vehicle to carry out his plans.

Tracking stations on earth — if he is within radio range — may follow his flight. They also know where his target is. Their computers use this information to figure his course corrections, then radio these commands to his vehicle's controls or display them on a panel before him. World-wide, there always is a station which has him "in view."

Space flight launch, control and tracking network

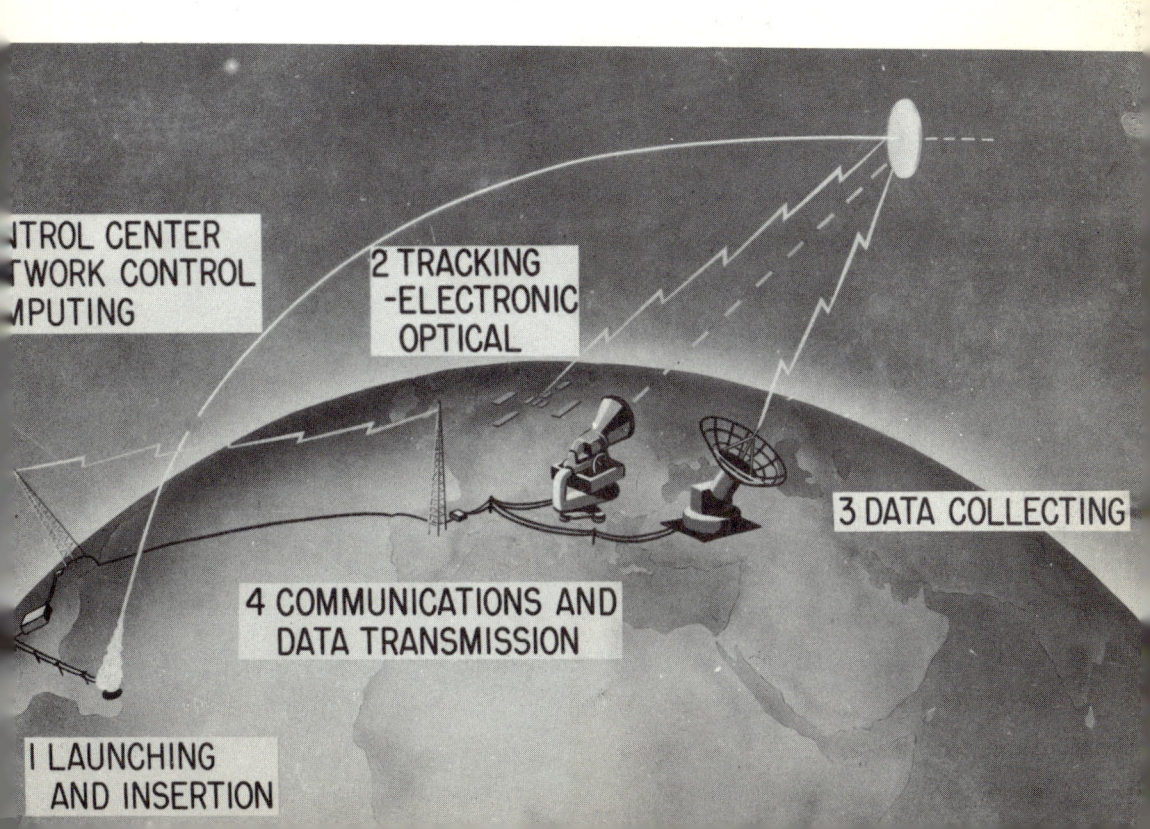

Inside a tracking and control station

If the astronaut is to rendezvous with an orbiting space station, his own craft may have to orbit several times first. Each orbit comes closer to the orbit of the target space station. To do this, he maneuvers his spacecraft to get its direction just right. Now he can put his craft on a transfer ellipse — transferring from one elliptical orbit to another. He engages his attitude hold — the control which automatically keeps his spacecraft in this new direction. Then he applies thrust. His craft transfers into its new orbit.

He does not "steer" his craft in the way that an airplane pilot does. Rather, he jockeys it. He aligns it so that it points in the direction — and that includes "up" and "down," as well as "right" or "left" — which he wants. But that direction is not in a straight line. It is a long curve, a part of another, new orbit. Somewhere on that curve, at a point far ahead in space predicted by his computer, his craft will intercept the target, the space station — which is traveling in orbit on a long curve, too.

To accomplish the transfer, the astronaut may have to make several earth orbits, but even with this "delayed rendezvous"

Rendezvous with overhead space station

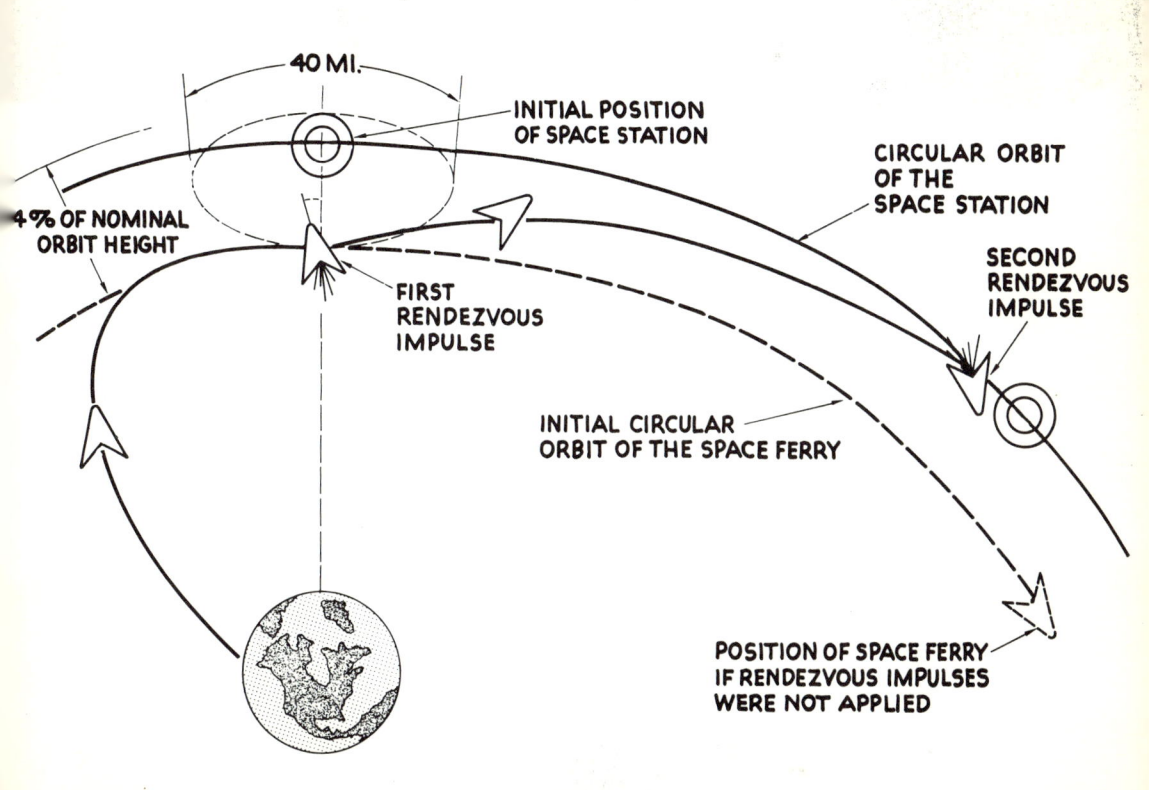

Transfers completed, the docking phase brings the spacecraft closer to rendezvous with the space station.

he finally enters into the homing phase; now he is only some twenty miles from target, in the same orbit, and at almost the same speed. He has already aligned, by his control grip, his vehicle to this new attitude at the end of the transfer. A brief application of thrust to his retro-rockets — and he reduced his closing rate.

Only a few hundred feet now separate his craft from the space station he has been watching on his radar screen or, perhaps on infra-red which "sees" even in the dark. Now he must carefully execute the delicate docking maneuver that will bring his craft to a safe coupling with the target. And here he can do better than a group of automatic machines. Very carefully he works the transfer control grip to change velocity, and the attitude control grip. In answer, the small rockets around his

The astronaut executes the docking maneuver that will bring his craft to a safe coupling with the target.

craft near its tail — the vernier rockets — issue little bursts of thrust, until his last fine adjustment brings the craft fast to the space station.

Aboard the space station are other astronauts, the crew. Depending upon their mission, there may be only two or three — or there may be as many as fifteen.

They do more than just keep their space station in its correct attitude in orbit. This may be a fueling station, or a space laboratory, or a weather observation station. Out here in space, the crew conducts experiments and makes telescopic observations which cannot be done on earth. Out here, far above earth's murky atmosphere, a telescope shows clearly the details of distant planets where future space missions will go.

Out here, other astronauts — for deep-space missions — get their advanced training. Here in space they learn the strange feel of space — weightlessness, and the meeting of no resistance to the action of arm or leg.

Here, too, they send unmanned space probes, or launch long-range spacecraft after these have been lofted from earth and then refueled in space. Here is no pull of gravity or drag of air against the departing craft; it attains its flight speed quickly, uses only a very little fuel. Its range is greatly increased.

Perhaps this particular space station's crew, instead of assisting in the training of astronauts or the launching of their deep-space ship, are the ones who refuel it. From their storage station, they pump fuel — or liquid oxygen — into the waiting tanks of

ESCAPE & REENTRY VEHICLE

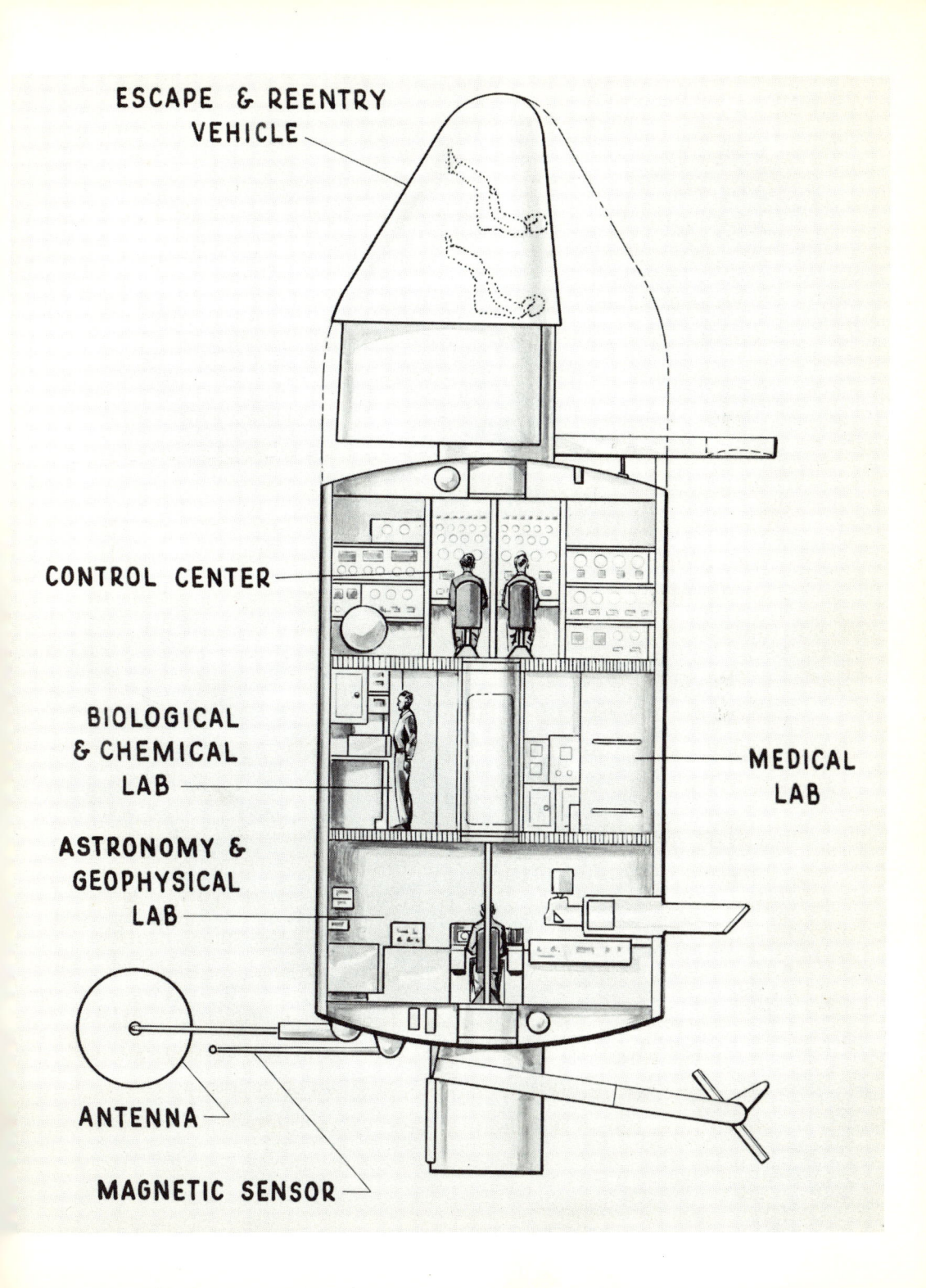

CONTROL CENTER

BIOLOGICAL & CHEMICAL LAB

MEDICAL LAB

ASTRONOMY & GEOPHYSICAL LAB

ANTENNA

MAGNETIC SENSOR

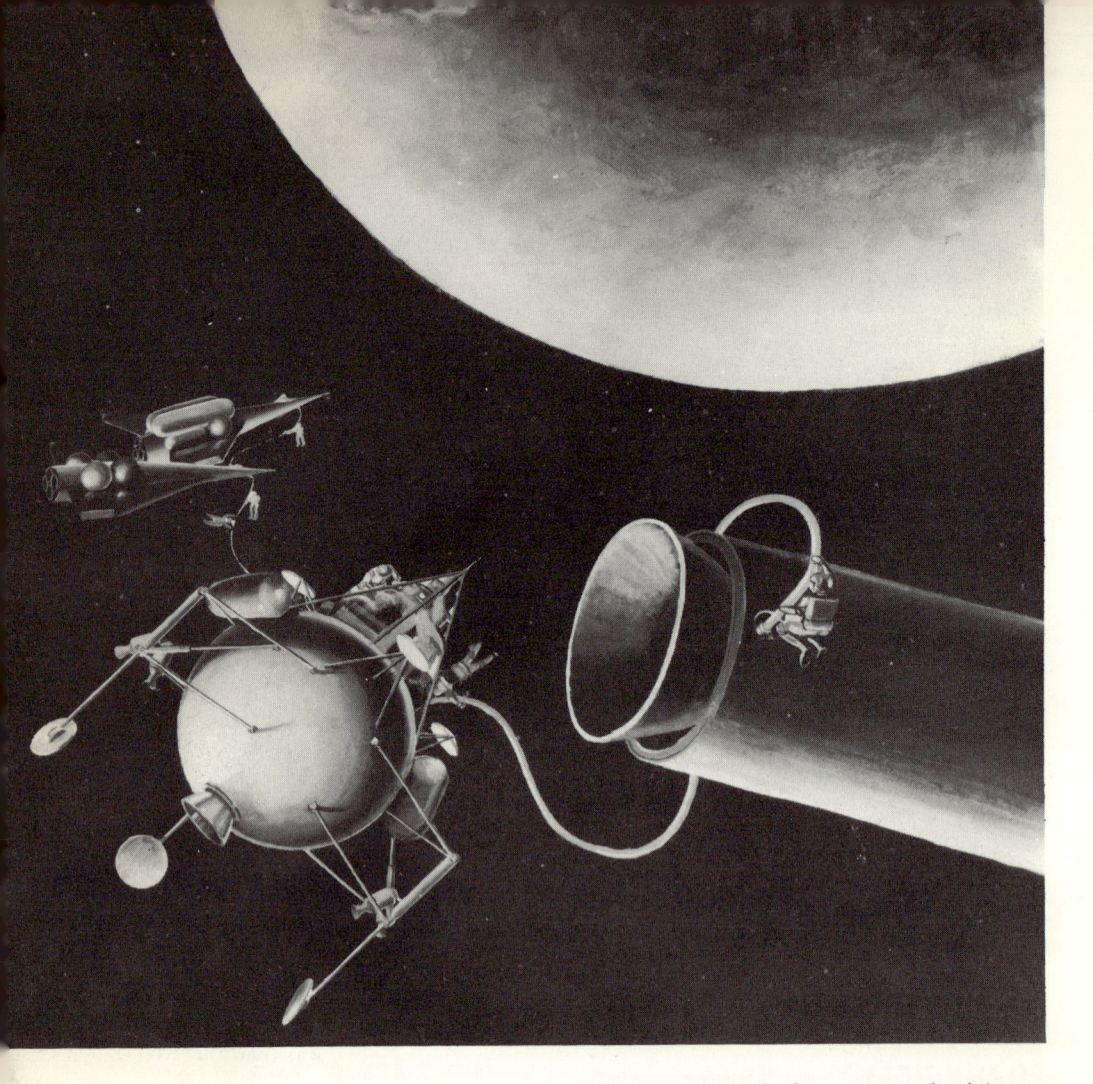

Space tanker refuels a spacecraft while two other craft prepare for re-entry to earth.

the spacecraft. Or, if theirs is another kind of fueling station, they just attach their station's tank to the spacecraft. The spacecraft had dropped off its emptied tanks while ascending and getting into orbit.

Escape capsule blasts from damaged space station, then retro-fires to decay its orbit and slow its descent.

All stations have either a commuter, or a return capsule or some sort of emergency craft, which the crew can use if their station is disabled. This is no more than a ship having lifeboats. But these space "lifeboats" must keep their crews alive, no

55

matter how far out their station may have been, until these men can reach earth or a safe base or until help can reach them. The astronauts' "lifeboats" must provide them enough oxygen and air pressure and food and water, and radio, too.

Aboard their space station, the crew should be not only safe but also comfortable — they will do better work. In larger stations, the men do not need to wear space suits. Where they sleep, insulation keeps out noise of their station's motors. Their compartments are ventilated and air-conditioned. They sleep in beds — even though they may have to fasten themselves in because they are weightless and so might float out of bed.

They work in shifts. The compartments where they work — galley, maintenance section with its tools, communications room — are ventilated and cooled. So, too, are the laboratories, if this is a space lab: the medical lab where they experiment with plant and animal life out here where there is no weight; the geophysics lab where they measure earth more accurately and test the strength of its electromagnetic field. And here they test equipment and materials — and themselves — to learn how well all will perform in later, very long-distance space flights which may take months or years of travel away from earth and home.

The information collected here — and from the radios of probes and craft they launched — is sent to earth where it is used to help in establishing another space station in orbit — this time, around another planet. For although the information gained is accurate, it is not enough — for a *landing* on that planet. They must be sure that their landing place is a safe one and that they can return from it.

MANNED SPACE LABORATORY

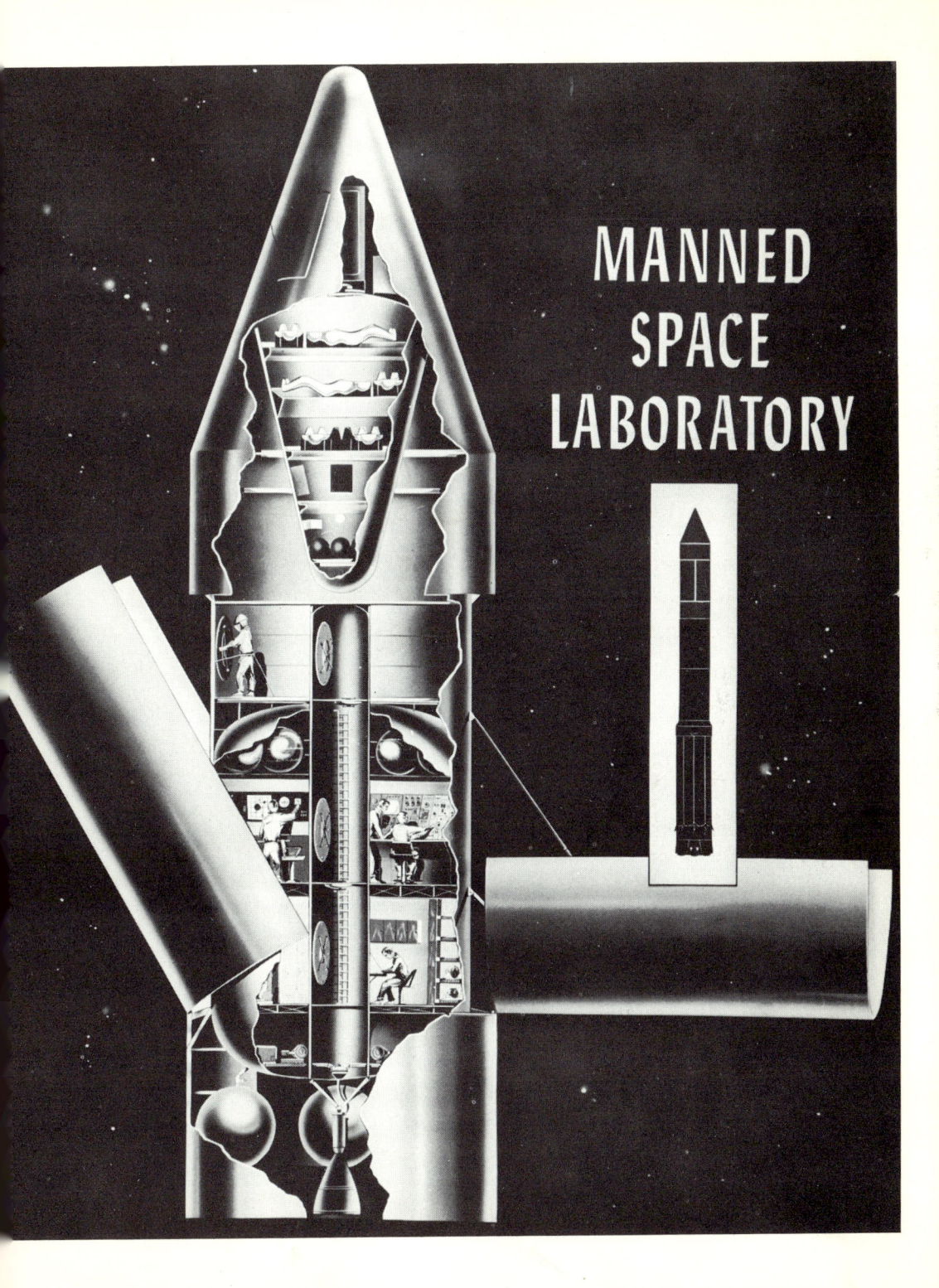

Crew of Mars-orbiting space station studies that planet's surface by telescope, radar and unmanned instrument probes.

And so the space station — their interplanetary spacecraft — orbits Mars, perhaps, while the astronauts aboard make their observations by telescope and radar. They send down probes equipped with TV and sensing devices; later, these probes are manned.

But before they attempt a landing on this strange planet, they return to earth. There, their new information goes into the making of new kinds of equipment needed for a landing under conditions never before experienced.

At last they are prepared to embark on this mission, to set foot on another world. A task force of two, or perhaps three, spacecraft sets out, navigates and journeys to this distant target, and takes up orbit around it. Now the crew — only as many as the mission needs — is ready.

They pass through the airlock of their craft into one of the commuters which each spacecraft brought along. Their pilot power-glides their commuter down in a long, shallow glide through the thin Martian atmosphere — careful not to generate too much heat, even though Mars' atmosphere is so much thinner than earth's.

Probe televises moon's surface to earth.

They land safely at their chosen site. Clad in special suits resembling their space suits, they leave their craft, and explore. They sample at firsthand the soil and moisture and atmosphere and plant life which their earlier radio probes reported. Above them orbit the other ships of the task force, their crews ready to rescue them, if need be.

When information about this new planet is complete enough, new crews will arrive and establish a base. An *extraterrestrial* base — beyond the earth.

BASIC REQUIREMENTS FOR SELF-SUPPORTING STRATEGIC LUNAR BASE
- OXYGEN • STRUCTURAL METALS OR CONCRETE • WATER
- FOOD • ELECTRIC POWER • OTHER BASIC RAW MATERIALS
- ADEQUATE CAPITAL EQUIPMENT • U^{235} • ROCKET FUEL

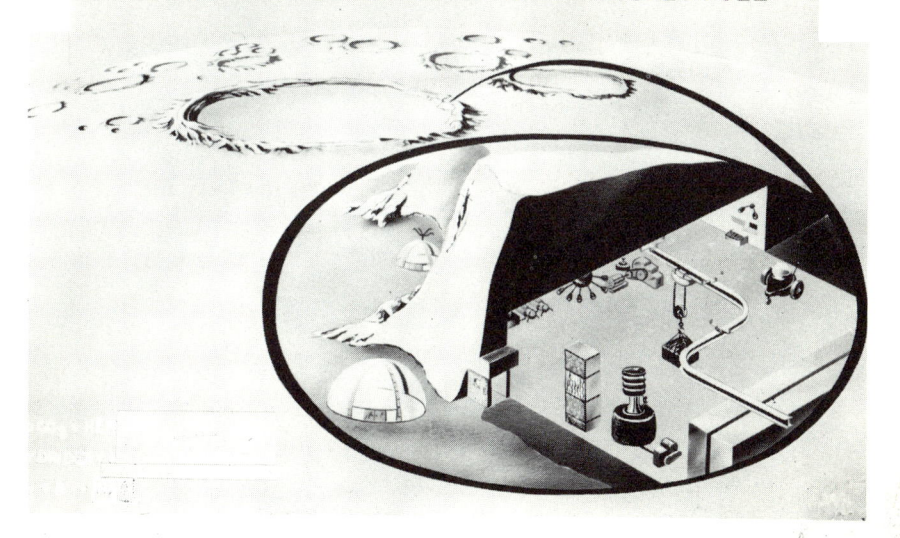

But their first extraterrestrial base was on the moon. It taught them a great deal. They use that information now in establishing this more distant base. On the moon they built a power station whose generators got their energy directly from the sun, and in the vacuum which the moon's surface provided. There, too, they built the base to manufacture its own air and provide them their food and water. And from that low-gravity base they were able to launch other deep-space flights — it made a fine take-off station for interplanetary flights. There were observatories, which could support bigger and more powerful equipment than could the earlier space stations; and these yielded still more information about that distant planet where a landing was to be attempted.

All the lessons learned earlier — in space station, in spacecraft, on the moon — are useful now: how to work in zero-gravity or low gravity, how to construct a space suit which lasts and is comfortable for a long time, how to provide food — and eat it — while weightless or almost so. Accurate navigation in space and in space conditions. Communications. Telemetering of information — automatically, by radio. And now that supply craft must deliver their cargo down through the atmosphere of this distant planet, the early lessons of bringing

A lunar colony, with its own manufactured atmosphere

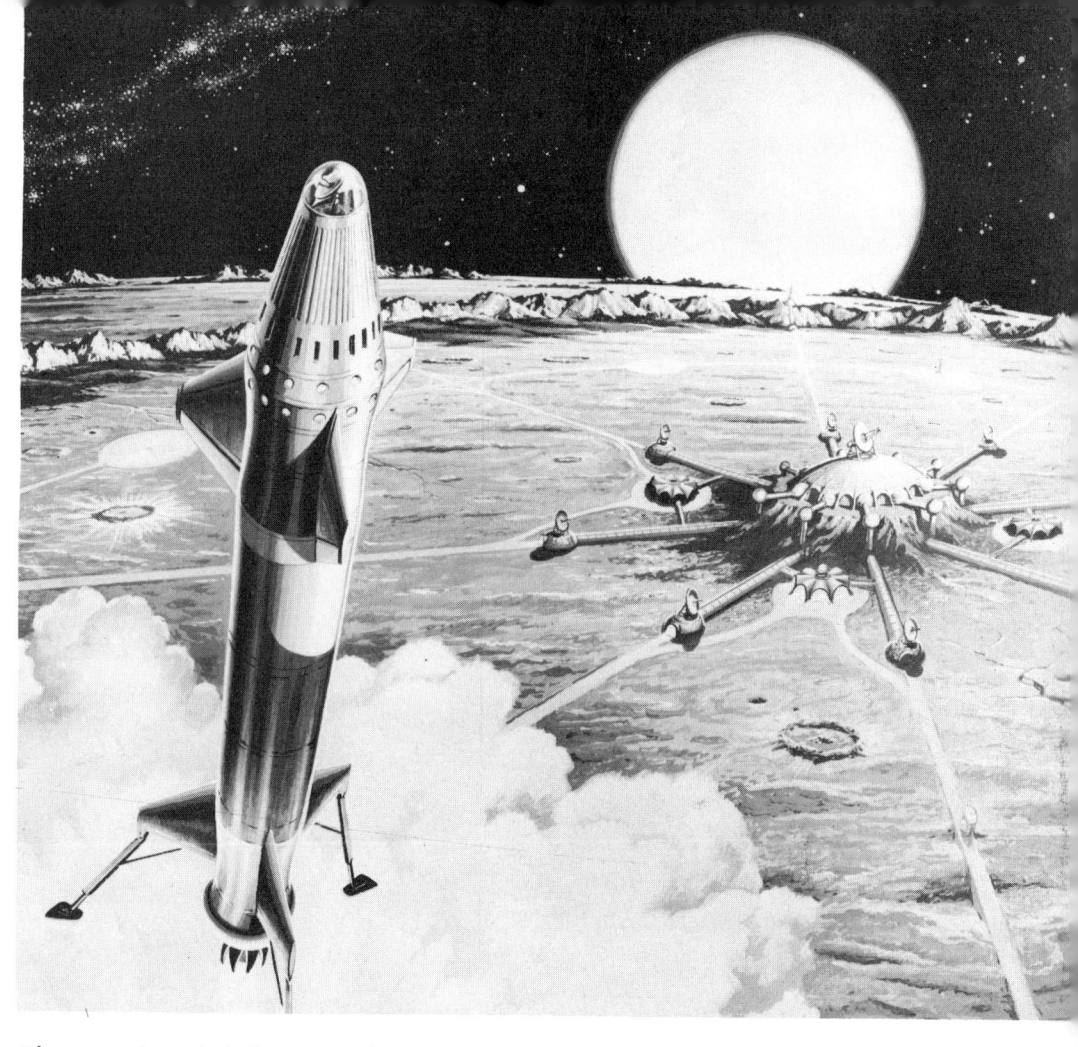

The moon base is built to manufacture its own air and provide food and water.

a spacecraft safely into re-entry — without burning up like a meteor — also help make this new venture a success.

From this new base the astronauts, and the specialized scientists they bring there, send back information which benefits all. These men who venture into space lead the way into the future.

An unmanned instrumented package impacts on the moon, to radio its findings to earth.